BrightRED Study Guide

Curriculum for Excellence

N5

GERMAN

Susan Bremner

BrightRED
PUBLISHING

First published in 2015 by:
Bright Red Publishing Ltd
1 Torphichen Street
Edinburgh
EH3 8HX

Reprinted with corrections 2018

A CIP record for this book is available from the British Library

ISBN 978-1-906736-54-5

With thanks to:
PDQ Digital Media Solutions Ltd, Bungay (layout), Anna Stevenson (copy-edit) and Carolin Zywotteck (German language check)

Cover design and series book design by Caleb Rutherford – e i d e t i c

Acknowledgements
Every effort has been made to seek all copyright-holders. If any have been overlooked, then Bright Red Publishing will be delighted to make the necessary arrangements.

Permission has been sought from all relevant copyright holders and Bright Red Publishing are grateful for the use of the following:

Permission has been sought from all relevant copyright holders and Bright Red Publishing are grateful for the use of the following:

Wavebreakmedia/iStock.com (p 6); barsik/iStock.com (p 8); Tomwang112/iStock.com (p 9); AlexRaths/iStock.com (p 10); YanLev/iStock.com (p 10); andresrimaging/iStock.com (p 10); Sintez/iStock.com (p 12); Benford Terex (p 14); shironosov/iStock.com (p 15); gpointstudio/iStock.com (p 15); Image licensed by Ingram Image (p 15); KatarzynaBialasiewicz/iStock.com (p 15); uriy2007/iStock.com (p 15); CREATISTA/iStock.com (p 15); Portra/iStock.com (p 15); CharlesKnox/iStock.com (p 15); Wavebreakmedia/iStock.com (p 15); Images licensed by Ingram Image (pp 16, 47, 51 & 72); Carissa Rogers (CC BY 2.0)1 (p 17); Africa Studio/Shutterstock.com (p 18); amadea/iStock.com (p 18); szefei/iStock.com (p 18); JackF/iStock.com (p 18); igzz/iStock.com (p 18); DragonImages/iStock.com (p 18); AndreyPopov/iStock.com (p 18); monkeybusinessimages/iStock.com (p 18); USFS Region 5 (CC BY 2.0)1 (p 18); hxdyl/iStock.com (p 18); Elenathewise/iStock.com (p 18); kzenon/iStock.com (p 18); tilo/iStock.com (p 18); serezniy/iStock.com (p 18); Pepe Pont (CC BY-ND 2.0)2 (p 20); Maksym Bondarchuk/Dreamstime.com (p 22); Image licensed by Ingram Image (p 22); Lorelyn Medina/Shutterstock.com (p 24); Lisa F. Young/Shutterstock.com (p 24); conrado/Shutterstock.com (p 24); Sergey Nivens/Shutterstock.com (p 24); Sam72/Shutterstock.com (p 24); ollyy/Shutterstock.com (p 24); iQoncept/Shutterstock.com (p 24); Barnaby Chambers/Shutterstock.com (p 24); Aleksandr Bryliaev/Shutterstock.com (p 24); Derrick Austinson Photog (CC BY-SA 2.0)3 (p 24); Countdown Studio (public domain) (p 24); Oleg Zabielin/Shutterstock.com (p 24); Andrew Moore (CC BY-SA 2.0)3 (p 24); iQoncept/Shutterstock.com (p 24); Jetrel/Shutterstock.com (p 24); Imagestate (p 25); pxel66/iStock.com (p 27); Image licensed by Ingram Image (p 31); NataliTerr/Shutterstock.com (p 32); monokini/freeimages.com (p 32); hartini a/FreeImages.com (p 34); BrianAJackson/iStock.com (p 36); Golf Resort Achental Team (CC BY 2.0)1 (p 38); Caleb Rutherford e i d e t i c (pp 38 & 52); Makhnach_S/Shutterstock.com (p 39); mhx (CC BY-SA 2.0)3 (p 42); S.Borisov/Shutterstock.com (p 44); Natalia Klenova/Shutterstock.com (p 44); Huguette Roe/Dreamstime.com (p 44); stephenmeese/iStock.com (p 47); vincentraal (CC BY-SA 2.0)3 (p 47); Syda Productions/Shutterstock.com (p 48); brown54486/iStock.com (p 48); monkeybusinessimages/iStock.com (p 48); Simone van den Berg/Shutterstock.com (p 47); wavebreakmedia/Shutterstock.com (p 48); shho/freeimages.com (p 50); monkeybusinessimages/iStock.com (p 52); CQYoung/iStock.com (p 54); lovleah/iStock.com (p 55); f9photos/iStock.com (p 56); Marcio Silva/iStock.com (p 57); ferlistockphoto/iStock.com (p 58); Austin Community College (CC BY 2.0)1 (p 60); AndreyPopov/iStock.com (p 60); mikeinlondon/iStock.com (p 60); Smokhov/iStock.com (p 62); gehringj/iStock.com (p 63); gpointstudio/Shutterstock.com (p 64); Sergey Nivens/Shutterstock.com (p 64); AfricaImages/iStock.com (p 65); CandyBox Images/Shutterstock.com (p 66); Andrey_Popov/Shutterstock.com (p 64); monkeybusinessimages/iStock.com (p 64); Jieyu Lai/Dreamstime.com (p 67); Poprotskiy Alexey/Shutterstock.com (p 72); Ryan Rutherford (p 72); Oiva Eskola (CC BY 2.0)1 (p 74); Makhnach_S/Shutterstock.com (p 75); Bryan Ledgard (CC BY 2.0)1 (p 78); filmfoto/iStock.com (p 79); bluestocking/iStock.com (p 86); Rawpixel Ltd/iStock.com (p 87); Image licensed by Ingram Image (p 88);

1(CC BY 2.0)   http://creativecommons.org/licenses/by/2.0/
2(CC BY-ND 2.0) http://creativecommons.org/licenses/by-nd/2.0/
3(CC BY-SA 2.0) https://creativecommons.org/licenses/by-sa/2.0/

Printed in the UK.

CONTENTS

INTRODUCTION

INTRODUCING NATIONAL 5 GERMAN

During this course, you will further develop your linguistic knowledge and will build up learning skills that will be useful beyond the exam environment. Learning any language will help you to develop your literacy skills both in the foreign language and in English, and will allow you to improve your knowledge about the culture of other countries.

THE NATIONAL 5 GERMAN COURSE

National 5 German encourages you to become a more confident learner; a responsible citizen with an informed and ethical view of other cultures and traditions in German-speaking countries; and someone who can work independently as well as participate in group discussions and team work.

COURSE ASSESSMENT

The course assessment at National 5 has five components as outlined in the table below.

Component	Mark	Scaled Mark	Duration
Component 1: question paper 1 Reading	30	30	1 Hour and 30 minutes (for paper 1 – Reading and Writing)
Component 2: question paper 1 Writing	20	15	See above
Component 3: question paper 2 Listening	20	30	Approximately 30 minutes
Component 4: assignment – Writing	20	15	No set time limit – centres to use their discretion
Component 5: Performance – Talking	30	30	Approximately 6–8 minutes

COMPONENT 1, 2 AND 3: READING AND WRITING; LISTENING

In these components, you will be assessed on all four contexts: society, learning, employability and culture. The question papers for Components 1, 2 and 3 are set and marked by SQA and conducted in your school/college/university under exam conditions in either May or June.

QUESTION PAPER 1 – READING AND WRITING (50 MARKS)

This question paper will assess the skills of reading and writing. The question paper will have two sections:

- reading – 30 marks
- writing – 20 marks, scaled mark 15.

Section 1 (reading)

You will read three texts and demonstrate your understanding by providing answers in English to the questions asked.

Each text will be based on one of the four contexts (society, learning, employability, culture), and all the texts will be of equal length and difficulty.

This section is worth a total of 30 marks, with each text being worth 10 marks. There will be 1–2 supported marks in each text, with one out of the total 3–6 supported marks being an overall purpose question.

There will be a variety of question styles, and you will be allowed to use a dictionary.

Section 2 (writing)

You will be required to write an e-mail of 120–150 words in German in response to a job advert. There will be four predictable bullet points and two less predictable bullet points. You should have prepared for this thoroughly beforehand and should feel fully equipped to tackle this paper. You will, however, be allowed to use a dictionary.

For help with this section, refer to pp. 82–89 of this book.

contd

QUESTION PAPER 2 – LISTENING (20 MARKS, SCALED MARK 30)

You will listen to one monologue in German worth 8 marks and one short conversation in German worth 12 marks. You will demonstrate your understanding by providing short answers in English to the questions asked.

This paper will be based on the context which was not covered in Question paper 1, for example if the reading texts cover society, culture and learning then the listening paper will be on employability.

This paper is worth a total of 20 marks and there will be a total of 2–3 supported marks, one of which will be in the monologue and will relate to the speaker's 'intent/reason/attitude/opinion'.

Read about Components 4 and 5 on pp. 80–81 of this book.

HOW THIS BOOK CAN HELP YOU

BrightRED Study Guide: National 5 German focuses on your work in the year leading up to the examination. It provides you with a complete study toolkit to take you through the National 5 course topic by topic, allowing you to develop your language skills and acquire effective techniques for handling exam questions. You will learn a range of ways to revise, either on your own or with friends.

CHAPTER 1: SOCIETY	CHAPTER 2: LEARNING	CHAPTER 3: EMPLOYABILITY	CHAPTER 4: CULTURE	CHAPTER 5: WRITING
Society covers the language needed to discuss relationships with family and friends; healthy lifestyles and illnesses related to a unhealthy lifestyle; the media and the impact of reality TV and new technology on our lives; citizenship and the importance of learning foreign languages; the environment and the differences between town and country life and your local area as a tourist centre.	Learning covers the language needed to discuss education and exam preparation; different education systems and responsibilities of learners.	Employability covers the language needed to discuss different jobs, including part-time work; covering letters, CVs and job applications and reviewing achievements and evaluating experiences.	Culture covers the language needed to discuss your best holiday/trip; the importance of travelling; aspects of other countries, including special events and occasions and literature/films.	Writing covers the language you will need to allow you to feel fully prepared for the Writing paper in the exam. This includes personal details (name, age, where you live); school/college education experience until now; skills/interests you have which make you right for the job; related work experience and possible examples of the two unpredictable bullet points.

Beyond the exam

Not only will this book help you to prepare for and do well in National 5 German, it will also help lay down the skills you will need to do well next year if you decide to continue with Higher German or study a new foreign language at Higher or National 5, take Modern Languages for Work Purposes Units, go into further study or training, or simply continue into the world of work.

THINGS TO DO AND THINK ABOUT

Whilst covering the context and topics in each chapter, you will develop your language skills, increase your vocabulary and be given the opportunity to revise grammatical structures. After each topic, you will be asked to use the language learned to write a short essay about the topic. This should help you to consolidate what you have just learned; and you may also wish to use these essays to help prepare your Performance (talking) as part of the external examination.

DON'T FORGET

It is now up to you. We hope this book will prove useful and help to prepare you fully for both the Unit and Course assessments. Viel Glück!

ONLINE

The SQA website gives more detail on the grammar and topics that you will need to know about. Follow the link from www.brightredbooks.net/N5German

ONLINE

This book is supported by the BrightRED Digital Zone. Log in at www.brightredbooks.net/N5German to unlock a world of videos, links, tests and much more!

FAMILY AND FRIENDS – FAMILIE UND FREUNDE 1

FAMILY MEMBERS

 ACTIVITY: Hast du Geschwister? – Do you have any brothers or sisters?

What siblings do these people have?

1 Ich habe einen Stiefbruder.

2 Ich habe eine Halbschwester.

3 Ich habe einen jüngeren Bruder.

4 Ich habe eine ältere Schwester.

5 Ich habe einen Zwillingsbruder.

6 Ich habe eine adoptierte Schwester.

 ACTIVITY: Quiz: Wer ist das?

Can you remember the vocabulary in German for the various family members?

> **EXAMPLE:**
> der Vater deines Vaters = der Opa

1 der Bruder deines Vaters = ?

2 die Tochter deiner Mutter = ?

3 der Sohn deiner Tante = ?

4 die Schwester deiner Mutter =?

5 der Sohn deines Bruders =?

6 die Mutter deines Vaters = ?

FAMILY STATUS

It is important that you learn the following vocabulary about family status.

- ledig – single
- verlobt – engaged
- verheiratet – married
- getrennt – separated
- geschieden – divorced
- tot – dead

 ACTIVITY:

Translate the following sentences into English:

1 Mein Stiefbruder ist verheiratet und hat drei Kinder.

2 Meine Schwester ist ledig.

3 Mein Opa ist tot.

4 Meine Stiefschwester und ihr Mann sind getrennt.

5 Meine Kusine ist verlobt.

6 Mein Onkel und meine Tante sind geschieden.

DON'T FORGET

It is easy to confuse *die Geschwister* = brothers and sisters with *die Schwester* = sister

ONLINE

Try out the reading task on Geschwister at www.brightredbooks.net/N5German

DON'T FORGET

The most important rule when working through a reading text is to look for cognates – that is, words that look like English. *Kind* = kid = child, or *Eltern* = elders = parents

ACTIVITY: New type of family

Read this article from a German magazine about the new type of family in Germany, then answer the questions in English:

Nicht alle Kinder wohnen zusammen mit dem Vater und der Mutter. Es gibt viele Mütter oder Väter, die allein mit ihrem Kind zusammenleben. In einer großen Stadt wie München ist jede vierte Familie eine 'Mini-Familie'. Das bedeutet Mutter oder Vater und Kind. Viele Eltern trennen sich, weil es so viele Probleme im Haus gibt. Vielleicht hat ein Elternteil den Job verloren und es gibt Probleme mit dem Geld. Manchmal lieben die Eltern sich nicht mehr. Sie haben andere Interessen.

Oft heiratet der Vater eine neue Partnerin oder die Mutter einen neuen Partner. Der Partner oder die Partnerin bringt oft Kinder mit. Man muss das Haus mit einem Stiefbruder oder mit einer Stiefschwester teilen. Es ist nicht so einfach. Es gibt vielleicht nicht genug Platz im Haus. Dein Vater oder deine Mutter hat nicht genug Zeit für dich. Die Kinder sind oft traurig.

1 What is the definition of a mini-family?

2 How common are mini-families in Munich?

3 Give two reasons why parents might separate.

4 Mention two possible problems caused by having stepbrothers and stepsisters.

ONLINE

Need more practice? Try out the reading text on family life at www.brightredbooks.net/N5German

DESCRIBING FAMILY MEMBERS

When you are describing another person, the verb, as long as it is a regular verb, will end in 't':

EXAMPLE

Meine Mutter heiß**t** Helen.

Sie spiel**t** gern Tennis.

The two most common verbs used when describing people are *haben* = to have and *sein* = to be. Both these verbs are irregular and need to be learned by heart.

ONLINE

Find out more about *Verben* on www.brightredbooks.net/N5German

DESCRIBING SELF	DESCRIBING A MALE	DESCRIBING A FEMALE
ich **habe** braune Haare	er **hat** braune Haare	sie **hat** braune Haare
ich **bin** klein	er **ist** klein	sie **ist** klein

Note the words for his and her: *sein(e)* = his, *ihr(e)* = her.

EXAMPLE

Sein Geburtstag ist am vierten Mai. – His birthday is on 4 May.

Ihre Haare sind schwarz. – Her hair is black.

VIDEO LINK

Learn more about this topic by watching the clips at www.brightredbooks.net/N5German

THINGS TO DO AND THINK ABOUT

Copy out the following paragraph, choosing the correct option in each case. Then, using the text as a model, write a paragraph about your own family.

Ich habe eine/einen Bruder. Sie/Er heißt Florian. Sein/Ihr Geburtstag ist am vierten November. Ihre/Seine Haare sind braun. Mein/Meine Schwester ist sportlich. Ihr/Sein Lieblingssport ist Tennis. Sie/Er ist in einer Mannschaft. Mein/Meine Eltern sind streng. Sie/Er gehen gern wandern. Meine/Mein Oma wohnt mit uns. Er/Sie ist lustig. Sie kann ihre/seine Brille nie finden. Der/Die Hund heißt Max. Sie/Er ist groß und spielerisch. Sein/Ihr Fell ist braun und weiß.

ONLINE TEST

Take the test 'Can you remember all the endings for regular verbs and all the parts of haben and sein?' at www.brightredbooks.net/N5German

FAMILY AND FRIENDS – FAMILIE UND FREUNDE 2

WIE IST DEINE FAMILIE? – WHAT IS YOUR FAMILY LIKE?

Learning vocabulary

First, read through the following adjectives and cover up the English meanings. Put a tick beside the words you recognise. This might be because the word looks like an English word or because you have already learned the German word. Highlight the words you don't know. These are the words you should spend more time learning. Try making learning cards. Cut some paper or cardboard into card shapes and write the German word on one side and its English meaning on the other side. Try to remember what each German word means without having to flip the card to check.

You can listen to these adjectives online at www.brightredbooks.net/N5German to help you with the pronunciation.

Positive adjective	English meaning	Positive adjective	English meaning	Positive adjective	English meaning
ehrlich	honest	hilfsbereit	helpful	phantasievoll	imaginative
fleißig	hard-working	klug	clever	ruhig	quiet
geduldig	patient	kreativ	creative	selbstsicher	self-confident
gelassen	laid-back	lebhaft	lively	sympathisch	nice
gesellig	sociable	lustig	funny	unabhängig	independent
gut gelaunt	good-natured	mitfühlend	sympathetic	verständnisvoll	understanding

> **DON'T FORGET**
>
> A false friend is a word in German that looks like a word in English but means something different. For example, you might guess that sympathisch means 'sympathetic' as it looks similar, but it actually means 'nice'.

1   You could add in a qualifier to improve the sentence. Here are the most common qualifiers:

sehr = very   ganz = quite   ziemlich = quite   echt = really   wirklich = really

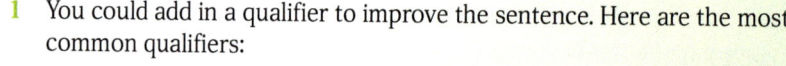

EXAMPLE:

Mein Bruder ist sehr lebhaft und ziemlich lustig. – My brother is very lively and quite funny.

It is important to avoid repetition, so make sure you use a variety of adjectives and qualifiers.

2   You can also add in a time phrase:

EXAMPLE:

Meine Schwester ist immer fleißig. – My sister is always hard-working.

Other time phrases you could use are:

manchmal = sometimes   oft = often   ab und zu = now and again
nie = never   selten = seldom

Now make use of your vocabulary-learning techniques to learn these negative adjectives. You can also listen to these adjectives online at www.brightredbooks.net/N5German to help you with the pronunciation.

Negative adjective	English meaning	Negative adjective	English meaning	Negative adjective	English meaning
angeberisch	boastful	frech	cheeky	schlecht gelaunt	bad-tempered
ärgerlich	annoying	gemein	mean/nasty	streng	strict
doof	stupid	kindisch	childish	traurig	sad
eingebildet	conceited	langweilig	boring	ungeduldig	impatient
ernsthaft	serious	launisch	moody		
faul	lazy	neidisch	envious		

ACTIVITY: Match up

Match up the German adjective with the English meaning.

1 ruhig	A childish
2 launisch	B cheeky
3 gemein	C nice
4 klug	D helpful
5 kindisch	E quiet
6 nett	F clever
7 frech	G moody
8 lustig	H hard-working
9 fleißig	I nasty
10 hilfsbereit	J funny

ACTIVITY: *Richtig* or *falsch*?

Are the following meanings *richtig* (true) or *falsch* (false)?

1 launisch = lovely
2 nett = nice
3 frech = friendly
4 lustig = funny
5 ruhig = quiet
6 streng = strong
7 doof = stupid
8 fleißig = flirty
9 gemein = nasty
10 klug = cute
11 hilfsbereit = helpful
12 kindisch = kind

ACTIVITY:

Translate the following German sentences into English.

1 Meine Oma ist sehr fleißig und ihr Haus ist immer ordentlich.
2 Mein Bruder ist besonders gesellig und hat einen großen Freundeskreis.
3 Meine Tante ist verständnisvoll und mitfühlend und sie hört sich meine Probleme immer an.
4 Mein Stiefbruder ist faul und hilft nie im Haus.
5 Meine Kusine ist ärgerlich denn sie muss die ganze Zeit reden.
6 Mein Opa ist immer lustig und erzählt gern Witze.
7 Meine Mutter ist meistens gut gelaunt denn sie denkt immer positiv.
8 Mein Onkel ist kreativ und phantasievoll und organisiert interessante Ausflüge für uns.

THINGS TO DO AND THINK ABOUT

Now use the knowledge you have gained in these pages to build better sentences.

1 Copy and complete the sentences with a time phrase: *manchmal, nie, oft*, and so on.
   a Meine Mutter ist _____ launisch.
   b Mein Opa ist _____ faul.
   c Mein Cousin ist _____ frech.
   d Meine Tante ist _____ gut gelaunt.
2 Copy and complete the sentences with a qualifier: *sehr, ganz, wirklich*, and so on.
   a Meine Kusine ist _____ sportlich.
   b Meine Oma ist _____ geduldig.
   c Mein Onkel ist _____ freundlich.
   d Meine Eltern sind _____ streng.
3 Copy and complete the sentences with a positive adjective: *freundlich, lustig*, and so on.
   a Mein Bruder ist frech aber_____.
   b Meine Nichte ist faul aber _____.
   c Meine Tante ist laut aber _____.

ONLINE

There are extra questions on this topic at www.brightredbooks.net/N5German

ONLINE TEST

Take the 'Negative and positive adjectives' test online at www.brightredbooks.net/N5German

VIDEO LINK

Learn more about German adjectives by watching the clips at www.brightredbooks.net/N5German

RELATIONSHIPS – DIE BEZIEHUNGEN

VERSTEHST DU DICH GUT MIT DEINER FAMILIE? – DO YOU GET ON WELL WITH YOUR FAMILY?

Positive Beziehungen

- Ich verstehe mich gut mit … – I get on well with …

- Ich komme gut mit … aus – I get on well with …

- Ich habe ein gutes Verhältnis zu … – I have a good relationship with …

Note that the word for 'my' changes depending on whether the noun that follows it is masculine, feminine or plural.

Masculine: Ich verstehe mich gut mit mein**em** Vater/Bruder/Onkel/Opa.

Feminine: Ich komme gut mit mein**er** Mutter/Schwester/Tante/Oma aus.

Plural: Ich habe ein gutes Verhältnis zu mein**en** Eltern/Geschwistern/Großeltern.

It is useful to be able to say **why** you get on well with family members and friends.

The easiest way to say why you get on well with family members is to make a sentence using the word for 'because' (weil) and one of the positive adjectives. However, you need to apply the word-order rule: there is a comma before 'weil', and the verb is sent to the end of the sentence.

Ich verstehe mich gut mit meiner Mutter, <u>weil</u> sie verständnisvoll <u>ist</u>.

Ich komme gut mit meinem Bruder aus, <u>weil</u> er immer lustig <u>ist</u>.

There are some more advanced phrases you can use in the following activity.

ACTIVITY: Match up

Read the following German phrases and match them to the English meanings. You can listen to these phrases online at www.brightredbooks.net/N5German to help you with the pronunciation.

1	Ich kann meine Probleme mit meinen Eltern besprechen.	A	My parents give me a lot of freedom.
2	Meine Eltern haben die gleichen Interessen.	B	My parents treat me like an adult.
3	Meine Eltern verstehen mich.	C	I can discuss my problems with my parents.
4	Meine Eltern haben viel Zeit für mich.	D	My parents have modern ideas.
5	Meine Eltern geben mir viel Freiheit.	E	My parents have the same interests.
6	Meine Eltern mögen meine Freunde.	F	My parents give me lots of pocket money.
7	Meine Eltern helfen mir mit den Hausaufgaben.	G	My parents understand me.
8	Meine Eltern behandeln mich wie einen Erwachsenen.	H	My parents have a lot of time for me.
9	Wir unternehmen viel zusammen.	I	My parents help me with my homework.
10	Meine Eltern haben moderne Ideen.	J	We do lots of activities together.
11	Meine Eltern geben mir viel Taschengeld.	K	My parents like my friends.

EXAMPLE

helfen   Meine Eltern helfen mir mit den Hausaufgaben.

         Mein Vater hilft mir mit den Hausaufgaben.

geben   Meine Eltern geben mir viel Freiheit.

         Meine Mutter gibt mir viel Freiheit.

ACTIVITY: Complete each sentence

Complete each sentence with the correct verb in each case. Choose from:

hat/haben   gibt/geben   hilft/helfen

1 Meine Eltern _____ mir viel Taschengeld.
2 Meine Eltern _____ viel Zeit für mich.
3 Mein Stiefbruder _____ mir mit den Hausaufgaben.
4 Meine Mutter _____ moderne Ideen.
5 Mein Vater _____ mir viel Freiheit.
6 Meine Geschwister _____ mir mit meinen Englischvokabeln.
7 Meine Eltern _____ wenige Hausregeln.
8 Meine Eltern _____ die gleichen Interessen.

THINGS TO DO AND THINK ABOUT

It is good to talk and write about other people in your assessments. It shows that you have an understanding of the different verb endings.

DON'T FORGET

When talking about both your parents, the verb is plural and ends in 'en'. When talking about one parent only, then the verb ends in 't'. Remember, however, that some strong verbs change in the third person. When you are describing someone else, there is often a vowel change.

ONLINE TEST

Take the 'Relationships' test online at www.brightredbooks.net/N5German to test your knowledge of this vocabulary.

ONLINE

Follow the link at www.brightredbooks.net/N5German for more on relationships.

VIDEO LINK

Check out the clip at www.brightredbooks.net/N5German

FAMILY CONFLICTS – STREIT MIT DER FAMILIE

GIBT ES OFT STREIT? – ARE THERE OFTEN ARGUMENTS?

Negative Beziehungen

You can start off your sentence in various ways. Listen to the audio track to hear how these phrases are pronounced.

- Ich verstehe mich nicht gut mit meinem Vater. I don't get on with my dad.

- Ich komme nicht so gut mit meiner Schwester aus. I don't get on very well with my sister.

- Ich kann meinen Bruder nicht leiden. I can't stand my brother.

- Mein Cousin ärgert mich. My cousin annoys me.

- Mein Stiefbruder geht mir auf die Nerven. My stepbrother gets on my nerves.

 **ACTIVITY**   *Richtig* or *falsch*?

Read the following statements and decide if they are *richtig* (true) or *falsch* (false) with regard to you and your parents:

1 Meine Eltern sind sehr streng.

2 Sie behandeln mich wie ein Kind.

3 Meine Eltern haben keine Zeit für mich.

4 Meine Eltern verstehen mich nicht.

5 Sie haben altmodische Ideen.

6 Meine Eltern kritisieren meine Kleidung und meine Freunde.

ACTIVITY   'Weil' clauses

Now join the starter phrase and reason together using a 'weil' clause. Remember that the verb (underlined) is **sent** to the end of the sentence.

1 Ich komme gut mit meiner Mutter aus. Sie <u>ist</u> geduldig und tolerant.

2 Ich mag meinen Bruder nicht. Er <u>geht</u> mir auf die Nerven.

3 Ich verstehe mich gut mit meinem Vater. Er <u>hilft</u> mir mit den Hausaufgaben.

4 Ich habe ein gutes Verhältnis zu meiner Oma. Sie <u>hat</u> immer Zeit für mich.

5 Ich komme gut mit meinen Eltern aus. Wir <u>haben</u> die gleichen Interessen.

6 Ich mag meine Eltern nicht. Sie <u>kritisieren</u> meine Kleidung.

7 Ich verstehe mich gut mit meinen Eltern. Sie <u>geben</u> mir viel Freiheit.

8 Ich verstehe mich nicht gut mit meinen Eltern. <u>Ich bekomme</u> wenig Taschengeld.

ACTIVITY: Match up

Match up the German words with the correct English meaning.

Wir streiten uns über ...	We argue about ...
1 das Taschengeld	A clothes
2 das Ausgehen	B my appearance
3 Kleidung	C pocket money
4 die Schulnoten	D going out
5 die Handykosten	E homework
6 die Hausarbeit	F mobile phone costs
7 die Hausaufgaben	G school grades
8 mein Aussehen	H housework

Using a 'wenn' clause

When you use 'wenn', the verb is sent to the end of the sentence:

Meine Mutter ärgert sich, wenn ...   My mum gets annoyed when ...
Mein Vater schimpft mit mir, wenn ...   My dad gives me a row when ...
Meine Eltern beschweren sich, wenn ...   My parents complain when ...

... ich mein Zimmer nicht <u>aufräume</u>.   I don't tidy my room.
... ich im Haushalt nicht <u>helfe</u>.   I don't help in the house.
... ich meine Hausaufgaben nicht <u>mache</u>.   I don't do my homework.
... ich meine Musik zu laut <u>spiele</u>.   I play my music too loudly.
... ich ständig am Handy <u>bin</u>.   I am constantly on my mobile.
... ich spät nach Hause <u>komme</u>.   come home late.

Now build three sentences about your own situation using the three starter phrases above.

DON'T FORGET

These phrases are good to use if you want to impress your teacher, because they require a 'wenn' clause.

ONLINE TEST

Take the 'Family conflicts' test online at www.brightredbooks.net/ N5German to test your knowledge of this vocabulary.

ACTIVITY: Arguing with parents

Read the German text and answer the questions in English:

1. What do teenagers mainly argue with their parents about?
2. What else do they sometimes argue about?
3. Mention two things that children want to do that parents are against.
4. When do teenagers get a row from their mother?
5. What are children often like if their parents are not strict?

Teenagers streiten sich oft mit ihren Eltern, meistens über Taschengeld, Hausarbeit oder Hausaufgaben – manchmal über das Ausgehen. Die Kinder wollen am Samstagabend bis Mitternacht ausgehen. Die Eltern sagen: nein. Die Kinder wollen mit Freunden auf Urlaub fahren. Die Eltern sagen: du bist zu jung.

Teenagers streiten am meisten mit der Mutter. Die Mutter schimpft, wenn das Kind das Schlafzimmer nicht aufräumt oder schlechte Schulnoten bekommt. Aber die Lehrer in der Schule finden strenge Eltern besser. Wenn die Eltern nicht streng sind, sind die Kinder oft frech und faul.

THINGS TO DO AND THINK ABOUT

A common question in the conversation section of the talking assessment is 'Gibt es oft Streit?'. Here are some suggestions for building an answer:

- Ich streite mich oft/manchmal/ab und zu mit meinen Eltern.
- Wir streiten uns über ... – We argue about ...
- Meine Mutter/Mein Vater kritisiert ...

VIDEO LINK

Learn more vocabulary about families at www. brightredbooks.net/ N5German

HOUSE RULES – DIE HAUSREGELN

SIND DEINE ELTERN STRENG? – ARE YOUR PARENTS STRICT?

Here are some ideas to help you build up your talking answer or your essay for the writing assessment.

> Meine Eltern sind sehr/ganz/wirklich streng.

Add in an opinion phrase:

> Ich finde, dass meine Eltern streng **sind**. – I think that …

Remember that 'dass' sends the verb to the end of the sentence!

> Ich würde sagen, dass meine Eltern sehr streng **sind**. – I would say that …

This is a good opportunity to use the modal verbs *dürfen* = to be allowed to and *müssen* = to have to.

 **ACTIVITY**   Rules

Listen to the audio track for the pronunciation.

a   What are these teenagers not allowed to do?

1   Ich darf keine Party geben.

2   Ich darf keine Süßigkeiten essen.

3   Ich darf nicht fernsehen.

4   Ich darf nicht Computerspiele spielen.

5   Ich darf kein Fastfood essen.

6   Ich darf nicht in die Disko gehen.

7   Ich darf meine Freunde nicht anrufen.

8   Ich darf nicht allein in die Stadt gehen.

9   Ich darf kein Piercing haben.

10   Ich darf nicht rauchen.

11   Ich darf keinen Alkohol trinken.

12   Ich darf meine Haare nicht färben.

13   Ich darf meine Kleidung nicht selbst kaufen.

14   Ich darf keine Drogen nehmen.

b   What do these teenagers have to do?

1   Ich muss mein Zimmer aufräumen.

2   Ich muss meine Hausaufgaben machen.

3   Ich muss im Haushalt helfen.

4   Ich muss das Auto waschen.

5   Ich muss das Abendessen kochen.

6   Ich muss den Hund füttern.

7   Ich muss auf meinen kleinen Bruder aufpassen.

8   Ich muss meine Oma besuchen.

⚙ ACTIVITY: Sind deine Eltern streng? Gibt es Regeln?

Build a German sentence for each picture, saying what you can and cannot do:

Ich darf ...   I am allowed to ...
Ich darf nicht + verb   I am not allowed to ...
Ich darf keinen/keine/kein + noun   I am not allowed ...

ONLINE

Head to the Digital Zone for an outline of commonly used modal verbs.

1
4
7

2
5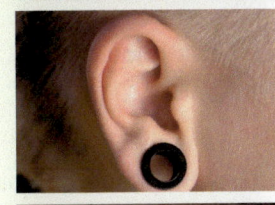
8

3
6
9

⚙ ACTIVITY: Missing words

Listen to the following text and try to fill in the missing words.

Ich wohne zu Hause _____ meinen Eltern. Eigentlich komme ich gut mit meinen Eltern aus. Sie _____ sich für mich und sie helfen mir, wenn ich Probleme in der _____ habe – ja, sie lieben mich. Aber meine Eltern lieben mich zu viel. Sie können nicht loslassen. Ich darf nie bei Freunden _____. Das finde ich unfair. Es gibt oft Ärger, wenn ich _____ mit Freunden ausgehen will. Meine Eltern haben immer _____, dass etwas Schlimmes passieren kann. Ich muss versprechen, dass ich spätestens um _____Uhr zurückkomme. Das ist oft peinlich. Wenn ich auf einer Party bin, muss ich immer als Erste nach Hause fahren. Es gibt bei uns immer _____, wenn ich spät nach Hause komme. Meine Freunde wollen alle in die Türkei in den _____ fahren. Ich glaube nicht, dass meine Eltern mir die Erlaubnis geben werden.

Schule   Angst   Urlaub   interessieren   Konflikte   elf   bei   abends   übernachten

VIDEO LINK

Check out the clips at www.brightredbooks.net/N5German to learn more.

⚠ THINGS TO DO AND THINK ABOUT

In talking and writing assessments, it is good to show that you can use modal verbs. You have just met dürfen and müssen. The other modal verbs are *können* = to be able to, *wollen* = to wish/want, *mögen* = to like and *sollen* = to ought to.

können ich kann   wollen ich will   mögen ich mag

ONLINE TEST

Take the 'Modal verbs' test online at www.brightredbooks.net/N5German to test your knowledge of this vocabulary.

EXAMPLE

Ich muss am Samstagabend um neun Uhr nach Hause kommen. Ich **kann** das nicht verstehen. Ich **mag** sehr gern tanzen und ich **will** länger in der Disko bleiben.

IDEAL PARENTS AND PEOPLE WHO INFLUENCE ME – IDEALE ELTERN UND LEUTE, DIE MICH BEEINFLUSSEN

IDEALE ELTERN – IDEAL PARENTS

Wie sind ideale Eltern?

It is usual to use the conditional tense when talking about ideal parents, since you are discussing a hypothetical situation.

In German, you would start the sentence with *ich würde ...* and place the main verb at the end of the sentence:

EXAMPLE:

Ich **würde** meine Kinder **lieben**.   I would love my children.

Ich **würde** meine Kinder **respektieren**.   I would respect my children.

 **ACTIVITY:** Ideal parents

Can you work out what these sentences mean?

1 Ideale Eltern würden geduldig und tolerant sein.

2 Ideale Eltern würden mir mit den Hausaufgaben helfen.

3 Ideale Eltern würden mir viel Freiheit geben.

4 Ideale Eltern würden keine Hausregeln haben.

5 Ideale Eltern würden moderne Ideen haben.

6 Ideale Eltern würden Zeit für ihre Kinder haben.

7 Ideale Eltern würden ihre Kinder nicht kritisieren.

8 Ideale Eltern würden meine Freunde akzeptieren.

9 Ideale Eltern würden kein Lieblingskind haben.

10 Ideale Eltern würden viel Taschengeld geben.

Now choose the five statements that you agree with the most and number them from 1 to 5, according to how important you consider each one to be.

ACTIVITY: Conditional tense

Try to translate the following sentences into German using the conditional tense:

1 I would talk to my children. (reden)

2 I would spend a lot of time with my children. (viel Zeit verbringen)

3 I would plan interesting activities for my children. (interessante Aktivitäten planen)

4 I would encourage my children. (ermutigen)

5 I would give my children advice. (Ratschläge geben)

ACTIVITY: What makes a good parent?

On a German website for teenagers, you come across the posts on the left about what makes good parents.

Mention two points made by each teenager.

Wie sind gute Eltern? Drei Jugendliche geben ihre Meinung dazu.

JULIA
Gute Eltern machen ihre Kinder glücklich. Glückliche Kinder sind nwormalerweise gesund und voller Energie. Gute Eltern setzen erreichbare Ziele, sonst werden die Kinder schnell enttäuscht.

MAXIMILIAN
Gute Eltern respektieren die Persönlichkeit ihres Kindes. Alle Kinder sind verschieden. Man darf sein Kind zwar auf seine Schwächen und Stärken hinweisen, muss sich aber auf die Stärken konzentrieren.

MORITZ
Gute Eltern unternehmen gemeinsam Dinge mit ihrem Kind. Sie reden jeden Tag mit ihm. Gute Eltern sollen auch mit den Hausaufgaben helfen.

LEUTE, DIE MICH BEEINFLUSSEN – PEOPLE WHO INFLUENCE ME

- Mein Vater hat mich viel beeinflusst. – My dad has influenced me a lot.
- Ich respektiere meine Mutter. – I respect my mum.
- Mein Großvater hat den größten Eindruck auf mich gemacht. – My grandad has had the biggest impression on me.
- Meine Oma spielt eine wichtige Rolle in meinem Leben. – My gran plays an important role in my life.
- Mein Bruder hat mir im Leben viel geholfen. – My brother has helped me a lot in life.
- Meine Schwester ist immer für mich da. – My sister is always there for me.
- Mein Onkel ist ein Vorbild für mich. – My uncle is a role model for me.

Here are some reasons why:

- Er/Sie hört immer gut zu. – He/She always listens.
- Er/Sie gibt gute Ratschläge. – He/She gives good advice.
- Er/Sie ist so lebenslustig. – He/She has such zest for life.
- Er/Sie hat eine positive Einstellung. – He/She has a positive outlook.
- Er/Sie kümmert sich um andere Leute. – He/She cares about others.

ONLINE

Go to www.brightredbooks. net/N5German for a Listening activity on this topic.

⚙ ACTIVITY: Grandparents

Read the German texts about the special role that grandparents play, and answer the questions in English, giving as much information as you can for each answer.

> Großeltern sind heutzutage sehr wichtig für viele Familien. Immer mehr Mütter gehen nach der Babypause zurück in den Job. Der Vater arbeitet auch den ganzen Tag. Niemand ist zu Hause. Kinderplätze kosten auch viel Geld, besonders wenn man mehrere Kinder hat. Ein Drittel aller Kinder unter sechs Jahren wohnen einmal in der Woche bei den Großeltern.

1 Why are grandparents very important for many families nowadays?
2 What statistic is given about grandparents and grandchildren?

> Omas und Opas kümmern sich im Durchschnitt 47 Stunden monatlich um ihre Enkelkinder. Die Beziehung zwischen Großeltern und Enkelkindern ist etwas besonderes. Die Großeltern sind oft nicht so streng und sie verwöhnen die Kinder. Die Kinder dürfen mehr Süßigkeiten essen oder später ins Bett gehen. Kinder lernen viel über ihre Familiengeschichte von den Großeltern. Sie finden heraus, dass der Vater sehr frech als Kind war oder dass die Mutter keine guten Schulnoten hatte.

3 Why is the relationship between grandparents and grandchildren often special?
4 What special treatment do grandchildren get?
5 What might children learn about their father and mother?

ONLINE TEST

Test your knowledge by taking the online listening test about people who influence you at www. brightredbooks.net/ N5German

THINGS TO DO AND THINK ABOUT

Personalise the sentences above to talk about people who have influenced you in your life. Do you spend much time with your grandparents?

DON'T FORGET

When doing a reading task, remember to work out the meanings of the nouns first. They are easily identified, as nouns are always written with a capital letter.

HOUSEWORK – DIE HAUSARBEIT

MUSST DU IM HAUSHALT HELFEN? – DO YOU HAVE TO HELP AROUND THE HOUSE?

This is a common question in talking assessments. Here are some phrases to help you build up your answer.

- Ich helfe viel im Haushalt. – I help a lot in the house.
- Ich helfe wenig im Haushalt. – I help little in the house.
- Mein Vater/meine Mutter macht die meiste Arbeit. – My dad/mum does the most work.
- Mein Vater/meine Mutter arbeitet viel und kommt spät nach Hause. – My dad/mum works a lot and comes home late.
- Er/sie ist müde nach einem langen Arbeitstag. – He/she is tired after a long day at work.
- Mein Bruder/meine Schwester tut nichts im Haushalt. – My brother/sister does nothing in the house.
- Es ist unfair. – It is unfair.
- Bei uns helfen alle im Haushalt. Jedes Familienmitglied hat eine Aufgabe. – In our house, everyone helps. Every family member has a task.
- Wenn ich nicht im Haushalt helfe, bekomme ich kein Taschengeld. – If I don't help out in the house, I don't get any pocket money.

⚙ ACTIVITY Household chores

Write down the correct German phrase for the household chore in each picture:

1
2
3
4
5
6
7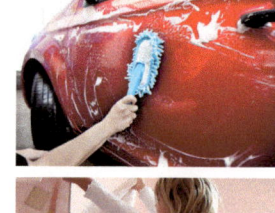
8
9
10
11
12
13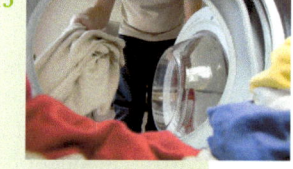
14

Ich mache mein Bett.	Ich wasche die Kleidung.	Ich koche das Abendessen.
Ich wasche ab.	Ich sauge Staub.	Ich decke den Tisch.
Ich bügele.	Ich räume mein Zimmer auf.	Ich wasche das Auto.
Ich füttere den Hund.	Ich giesse die Blumen.	Ich gehe einkaufen.
Ich arbeite im Garten.	Ich mähe den Rasen.	

 **ACTIVITY:**

Here are some good time phrases to use:

manchmal = sometimes, oft = often, ab und zu = now and again, nie = never, jeden Tag = every day

DON'T FORGET

Note that the time phrase comes after the verb.

 **ACTIVITY:** Sentence-builder

Build better sentences by completing each sentence about yourself with a time phrase:

1 Ich räume _____ mein Zimmer auf.
2 Ich mache _____ mein Bett.
3 Ich decke _____ den Tisch.
4 Ich bügele _____.

 **ACTIVITY:** Housework survey

The teenage magazine *Bravo* conducted a survey with teenagers about housework. The article below outlines the main findings of the survey. Read the German text and answer the questions in English:

Wir haben mit Schülern im Alter von 14 Jahren gesprochen. Lies die Fragen und das Ergebnis unserer Umfrage!

Wie viel hilfst du im Haushalt?

Fast die Hälfte hilft ab und zu am Wochenende, etwa ein Viertel hilft auch wochentags ungefähr eine halbe Stunde und einige helfen sogar ein bis zwei Stunden pro Tag. Eine kleine Anzahl von Schülern muss überhaupt nicht helfen.

Welche Arbeit machst du am meisten?

Zimmer aufräumen steht für die meisten an erster Stelle, gefolgt von Betten machen. Viele müssen auch den Tisch decken und abräumen. Abwaschen und Putzen stehen an vierter Stelle, aber Kochen ist keine sehr beliebte Arbeit.

Findest du, dass Kinder im Haushalt helfen sollen?

Die meisten Schüler meinen, dass Kinder ab zehn Jahren helfen sollen. Einige sagen, dass man helfen soll, so oft die Eltern wollen, aber fast alle finden eine halbe Stunde pro Tag richtig. Und alle sagen, dass Hausaufgaben wichtiger sind.

Findest du, dass Kinder für Hausarbeiten Geld verdienen sollen?

Fast niemand bekommt Geld für Hausarbeiten, und niemand ist darüber unglücklich. Die meisten finden, dass Hausarbeit zum Familienleben gehört. Die Ausnahme: Wenn man sonst kein Taschengeld bekommt oder wenn man sehr viel im Haushalt hilft, sollen die Eltern dafür bezahlen.

1 Complete the sentences:
   Almost half of the pupils help _____.
   _____ help on a weekday for roughly half an hour.
2 What are the two most popular chores?
3 How much time should children spend doing housework?
4 Most children do not get paid for household chores. When is this considered unacceptable?

 ONLINE TEST

Test your knowledge of household chores at www. brightredbooks.net/N5German

 THINGS TO DO AND THINK ABOUT

Write a paragraph discussing how household chores are divided up in your house. What housework tasks do you like/dislike? Do you think you should get paid for doing housework? Use the above text for ideas.

 VIDEO LINK

Head to www. brightredbooks.net/ N5German to watch the clip of a German girl talking about different household chores.

FRIENDSHIP – DIE FREUNDSCHAFT

HAST DU VIELE FREUNDE? – DO YOU HAVE LOTS OF FRIENDS?

Here are some useful phrases to help you build up a paragraph about friends:

- Ich habe viele Freunde (auf Facebook). – I have lots of friends (on Facebook).
- Sie sind keine echten Freunde. – They are not real friends.
- Ich habe einen großen Freundeskreis. – I have a big circle of friends.
- Ich bin in einer Clique. – I am in a gang.
- Ich habe ein paar gute Freunde. – I have a few good friends.
- Ich habe Freunde aus der Schule/ aus der Nachbarschaft/aus dem Sportverein/aus der Fußballmannschaft. – I have friends from school/from the neighbourhood/from the sports club/ from the football team.
- Wir treffen uns jeden Abend/jedes Wochenende. – We meet up every night/ every weekend.

- Wir gehen ins Kino zusammen. – We go to the cinema together.
- Wir spielen beide in dem Orchester. – We both play in the orchestra.
- Wir machen zweimal in der Woche Fitnesstraining zusammen. – We do a work-out together twice a week.
- Mein bester Freund/beste Freundin heißt ... – My best friend is called ...
- Wir kennen uns seit vier Jahren. – We have known each other for four years.
- Wir kennen uns seit der Grundschule. – We have known each other since primary school.
- Wir reden über Musik/Sport/Filme/ Freunde. – We talk about music/sport/ films/friends.

 **ACTIVITY** Match up 1

Match up: Ein guter Freund/eine gute Freundin ist ...

1 gut gelaunt	A helpful
2 lustig	B nice
3 hilfsbereit	C trustworthy
4 geduldig	D loyal
5 freundlich	E good-natured
6 nett	F lively
7 verständnisvoll	G patient
8 vertrauenswürdig	H understanding
9 treu	I funny
10 lebhaft	J friendly

ACTIVITY Sentence-builder

Build better sentences by adding in one of the words from the word bank for each blank:

1 Ein guter Freund ist _____ hilfsbereit.
2 Eine gute Freundin ist _____ geduldig.
3 Ein guter Freund ist _____ lustig.

4 Eine gute Freundin ist _____ verständnisvoll.
5 Wir reden über _____ und _____.
6 Wir streiten uns über _____ und _____.

Sport   sehr   immer   Musik   Fußball   wirklich   Geld   meistens

ACTIVITY: Match up 2

Copy out the German phrase, then try to find the correct English translation:

Ein guter Freund/eine gute Freundin …

hat immer Zeit für mich	is helpful and trustworthy
hat viel Geduld	has always got time for me
redet mit mir über alles	helps me when I have problems
gibt immer Unterstützung	has lots of patience
hat die gleichen Interessen	talks to me about everything
hilft mir, wenn ich Probleme habe	has the same interests
ist hilfsbereit und vertrauenswürdig	sticks by me
hält zu mir	is always supportive

ACTIVITY: Jan's friends

Read the German text and answer the English questions:

Ich bin der Jan. Meine Freunde sind wichtig für mich. Meine Freunde sind lustig und freundlich. Mein bester Freund heißt Thomas. Wir haben die gleichen Interessen. Wir lieben Sport, besonders Tennis. Wir sind in einem Klub und trainieren jeden Samstag. Wir reden oft über Musik und Computerspiele.

Manchmal streiten wir uns aber nicht oft. Mein Freund ist faul und unpünktlich. Wir kommen immer zu spät zur Schule. Er macht nie seine Hausaufgaben und nimmt mein Heft, so dass er abschreiben kann. Das ärgert mich.

1. What are Jan's friends like?
2. What does Jan have in common with his best friend?
3. Why do they sometimes argue?

MOBBING – BULLYING

ACTIVITY: Was ist deine Meinung?

Read each statement and write down your reaction:

Ich bin einverstanden = I agree   OR   Ich bin nicht einverstanden = I don't agree

1. Es gibt manchmal Gruppendruck.
2. Man muss in der Clique sein.
3. Man muss Markenkleidung tragen und Alkohol trinken.
4. Man muss sich schlecht benehmen, um den Respekt der anderen zu bekommen.
5. Man muss rauchen, um modisch und cool zu sein.
6. Es ist schwierig sich gegen die Gruppe zu stellen.

Now translate the sentences into English.

THINGS TO DO AND THINK ABOUT

Now write a paragraph about your friends. Do you have a best friend? What qualities do you look for in a friend? Have you ever been the victim of bullying?

ONLINE

Head to www.brightredbooks.net for a great activity on the subject of bullying.

ONLINE TEST

Complete the online test about friends at www.brightredbooks.net/N5German

VIDEO LINK

Check out the clip where a German girl narrates her experiences of bullying via a PowerPoint presentation at www.brightredbooks.net/N5German

DON'T FORGET

Remember that verbs are found in the infinitive form ending in 'en' in the dictionary, for example *drohen* = to threaten. You will need to use the irregular verb tables to find the other parts of each verb.

LEISURE – DIE FREIZEIT

WAS MACHST DU IN DEINER FREIZEIT? – WHAT DO YOU DO IN YOUR FREE TIME?

Here are some useful starter phrases:

- Meine Freizeit ist wichtig für mich. – My free time is important to me.
- Ich geniesse meine Freizeit. – I enjoy my free time.
- Ich freue mich immer auf das Wochenende. – I always look forward to the weekend.

Talking about what you do in your free time

The verbs you will use most often are *ich spiele* = I play and *ich gehe* = I go.

ICH SPIELE – I PLAY

Ich spiele – I play can be used with:

1 Sports

EXAMPLE:

Ich spiele Federball und Tischtennis. I play badminton and table tennis.

2 Musical instruments

EXAMPLE:

Ich spiele Gitarre. I play the guitar.

⚙ ACTIVITY Match up the instruments

1 Geige	5 Schlagzeug	A piano	E trumpet
2 Trompette	6 Dudelsack	B bagpipes	F recorder
3 Flöte	7 Klavier	C violin	G flute
4 Blockflöte		D drums	

3 Games

EXAMPLE:

Ich spiele Schach.   I play chess.

Ich spiele Karten.   I play cards.

Ich spiele Computerspiele.   I play computer games.

ICH GEHE – I GO

When do I use the verb *ich gehe*?

1 I go to + a place:

EXAMPLE

Ich gehe ins Kino.   I go to the cinema.

Ich gehe ins Schwimmbad.   I go to the swimming pool.

Ich gehe in die Eishalle.   I go to the ice-rink.

Ich gehe in die Stadt.   I go into town.

Ich gehe in das Jugendzentrum.   I go to the youth club.

Ich gehe auf Partys.   I go to parties.

contd

2 I go + an activity:

EXAMPLE

Ich gehe kegeln.	I go bowling.
Ich gehe einkaufen.	I go shopping.
Ich gehe reiten.	I go horse-riding.
Ich gehe wandern.	I go walking.

ACTIVITY: Hobby phrases

Here is a list of the other important hobby phrases that you will need to know. How often do you do these activities? Read each sentence, then choose a German time phrase to say how often you do the activity.

manchmal = sometimes   oft = often   selten = rarely   nie = never   jeden Tag = every day

1 Ich sehe fern.
2 Ich lese Zeitschriften/
   Bücher/Zeitungen.
3 Ich höre Musik/Radio.
4 Ich treibe Sport.
5 Ich faulenze.
6 Ich fahre Rad.
7 Ich koche.
8 Ich besuche meine Oma.
9 Ich bummele in der Stadt.
10 Ich mache meine
   Hausaufgaben.
11 Ich stricke.
12 Ich bastele.
13 Ich male.
14 Ich zeichne.

This is a good opportunity to put the word-order rules into practice. Here are two options:

a starting with a time phrase: the formula = time + verb + *ich* + rest of sentence

EXAMPLE

Am Samstag gehe ich in die Stadt.

b when + with whom + where

EXAMPLE

Ich gehe am Freitag mit meinen Freunden ins Kino.
Ich gehe jeden Sonntag mit meinem Cousin in die Eishalle.

THINGS TO DO AND THINK ABOUT

You could also say which activity you do depending on the weather. To do this, you will need to use a 'wenn' clause. When you start a sentence with 'wenn', the verb is sent to the end of the sentence. You end up with a verb, comma, verb situation.

EXAMPLE

Wenn es sonnig **ist, fahre** ich Rad.
Wenn es **regnet, gehe** ich ins Kino.

You can also write about the hobbies of friends and family. Remember that the verb ends in 't' when talking about someone else.

EXAMPLE

Mein Bruder spiel**t** Volleyball.
Meine Oma hör**t** klassische Musik.

ONLINE

Find more activities on hobbies at www.brightredbooks.net/N5German

DON'T FORGET

Remember the word for 'my' changes depending on whether the noun is masculine, feminine, neuter or plural.

VIDEO LINK

Learn more about the topic of leisure by watching the clips online at www.brightredbooks.net/N5German

ONLINE TEST

Take the hobbies online test at www.brightredbooks.net/N5German

TELEVISION – DAS FERNSEHEN

SIEHST DU VIEL FERN? – DO YOU WATCH A LOT OF TV?

The best way to build up a paragraph is to answer the 'w' questions:

When? Where? With whom? Why? What?

When? How long?

- Ich sehe ... fern – I watch TV
- Ich sehe nach der Schule fern. – I watch TV after school.
- Ich sehe nach dem Abendessen fern. – I watch TV after dinner.
- Ich sehe eine Stunde/zwei Stunden fern. – I watch TV for an hour/two hours.

Where?

- Ich sehe im Wohnzimmer fern. – I watch TV in the living room.
- Ich sehe in meinem Schlafzimmer fern. – I watch TV in my bedroom.
- Ich sehe bei meiner Oma fern. – I watch TV at my gran's house.

With whom?

- Ich sehe mit meiner Familie fern. – I watch TV with my family.
- Ich sehe mit meinen Freunden fern. – I watch TV with my friends.
- Ich sehe ganz alleine fern. – I watch TV on my own.

Why?

- Ich sehe fern, um mich zu entspannen. – I watch TV to relax.
- Ich sehe fern, um meine Probleme zu vergessen. – I watch TV to forget my problems.
- Ich sehe fern, um etwas zu lernen. – I watch TV to learn something.
- Ich sehe fern, um abzuschalten. – I watch TV to switch off.

⚙ ACTIVITY: What programme?

Write down the German word for the type of programme represented in the picture.

die Nachrichten   Natursendungen   Sportsendungen   Musiksendungen

Zeichentrickfilme   Seifenopern   Spielshows   Werbung   die Wettervorhersage

Komödien   Abenteuerfilme   Kriegsfilme   Krimis   Gruselfilme   Liebesfilme

1

4

7

10

13

2

5

8

11

14

3

6

9

12

15

EXPRESSING PREFERENCES AND OPINIONS

It is always good to express likes and dislikes:

- Ich liebe/Ich mag Zeichentrickfilme. – I love/like cartoons.
- Ich interessiere mich für/Ich sehe gern Natursendungen. – I am interested in/I like watching nature programmes.
- Ich hasse die Nachrichten/Ich mag die Nachrichten nicht. – I hate the news/I don't like the news.
- Ich kann Seifenopern nicht leiden/Ich sehe nicht gern Seifenopern. – I can't stand soaps/I don't like watching soaps.

You should try to give a reason as well as be able to express an opinion. Here are some adjectives you might use:

- spannend – exciting
- entspannend – relaxing
- kindisch – childish
- romantisch – romantic
- todlangweilig – really boring

- lehrreich – educational
- unterhaltsam – entertaining
- lustig – funny
- furchtbar/schrecklich – awful
- gruselig – scary

Giving a reason

> **EXAMPLE**
>
> Ich sehe gern Krimis, weil sie spannend sind.

Giving an opinion

> **EXAMPLE**
>
> Ich finde Zeichentrickfilme kindisch.
>
> Meiner Meinung nach sind Zeichentrickfilme kindisch.

 DON'T FORGET

When you talk about all programmes within a category, for example all detective programmes, then the plural form is used.

ACTIVITY: For or against TV

Are the following people for or against TV? Write down *für* (for) or *gegen* (against).

Now translate the sentences into English.

1 Das Fernsehen ist eine wichtige Informationsquelle.
2 Es gibt zu viel Werbung.
3 Viele Sendungen sind blöde.
4 Man lernt, was auf der Welt passiert.
5 Man kann sich entspannen.
6 Kinder sehen stundenlang fern. Sie sind zu passiv.
7 Man kann viel über eine andere Kultur lernen.
8 Man kann über die Sendungen reden. Es ist gesellig.
9 Es gibt zu viel Gewalt und Brutalität.
10 Man kann den Alltag vergessen.
11 Das Fernsehen ist wie eine Droge. Man wird schnell süchtig.
12 Man hört viele Schimpfwörter.

 ONLINE TEST

Try out the online test on TV at www.brightredbooks/N5German

VIDEO LINK

Check out the clips about television at www.brightredbooks/N5German

 ## THINGS TO DO AND THINK ABOUT

Write a paragraph in German about your TV-viewing preferences. Start with the 'w' questions, then go on to discuss your likes and dislikes, and finish by giving your opinion on whether you think TV is a good or bad mode of entertainment.

IS TV GOOD OR BAD FOR US? – IST DAS FERNSEHEN GUT ODER SCHLECHT FÜR UNS?

As well as saying what you watch on TV, it would be good to be able to discuss the positive and negative aspects of watching TV.

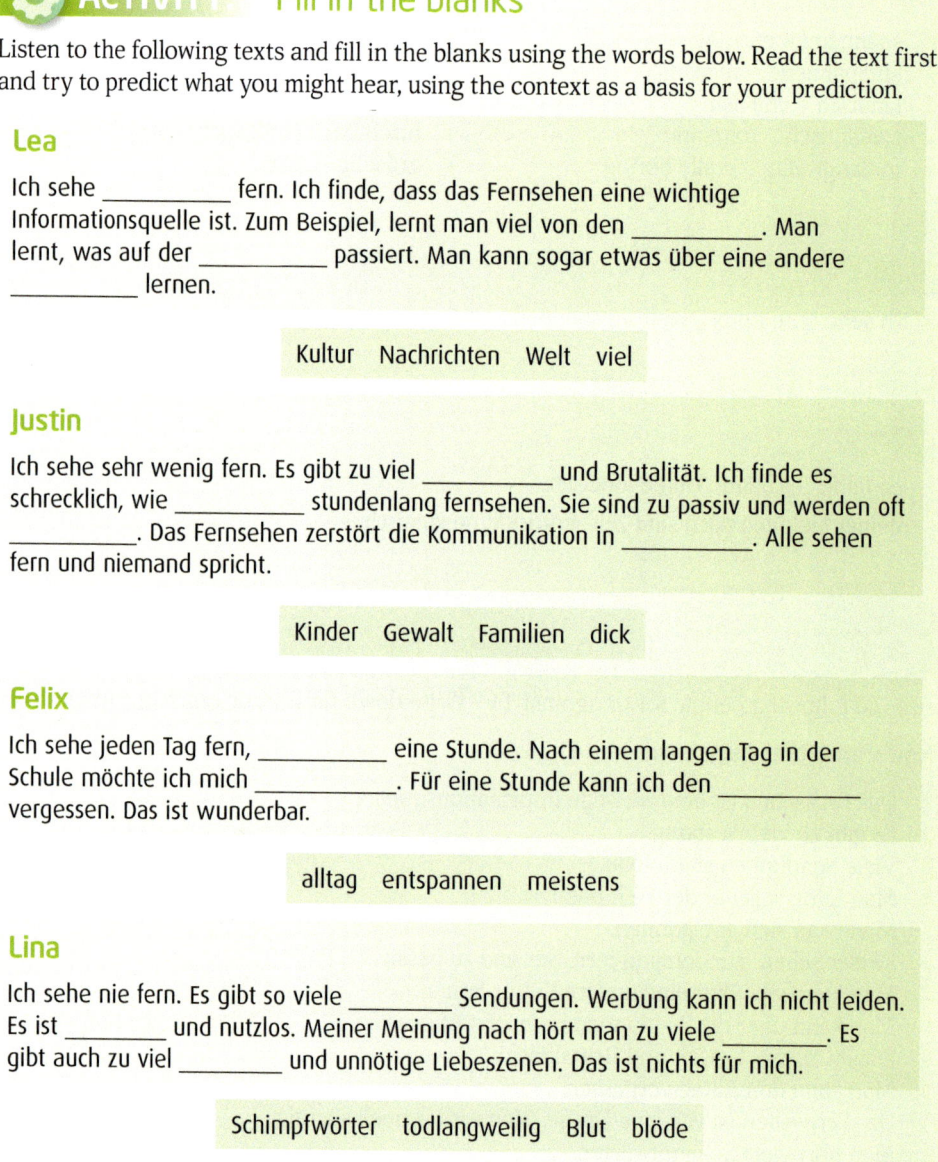

⚙ ACTIVITY: Fill in the blanks

Listen to the following texts and fill in the blanks using the words below. Read the text first and try to predict what you might hear, using the context as a basis for your prediction.

Lea

Ich sehe _____ fern. Ich finde, dass das Fernsehen eine wichtige Informationsquelle ist. Zum Beispiel, lernt man viel von den _____. Man lernt, was auf der _____ passiert. Man kann sogar etwas über eine andere _____ lernen.

Kultur   Nachrichten   Welt   viel

Justin

Ich sehe sehr wenig fern. Es gibt zu viel _____ und Brutalität. Ich finde es schrecklich, wie _____ stundenlang fernsehen. Sie sind zu passiv und werden oft _____. Das Fernsehen zerstört die Kommunikation in _____. Alle sehen fern und niemand spricht.

Kinder   Gewalt   Familien   dick

Felix

Ich sehe jeden Tag fern, _____ eine Stunde. Nach einem langen Tag in der Schule möchte ich mich _____. Für eine Stunde kann ich den _____ vergessen. Das ist wunderbar.

alltag   entspannen   meistens

Lina

Ich sehe nie fern. Es gibt so viele _____ Sendungen. Werbung kann ich nicht leiden. Es ist _____ und nutzlos. Meiner Meinung nach hört man zu viele _____. Es gibt auch zu viel _____ und unnötige Liebeszenen. Das ist nichts für mich.

Schimpfwörter   todlangweilig   Blut   blöde

REALITY TV – REALITY TV

⚙ ACTIVITY: Florian und Melanie sprechen über Reality TV

Read the conversation between Florian and Melanie where they discuss reality TV and answer the questions below.

contd

F Hast du die Reality TV Sendung *Ich bin ein Star – Holt mich hier raus!* gestern Abend gesehen? Es war so lustig – ich habe so gelacht und es hat mir sehr gut gefallen.

M Natürlich nicht! Ich kann solche Sendungen nicht leiden. Ich kann nicht glauben, wie beliebt diese Sendungen geworden sind. Sie sind zwecklos und haben nichts mit dem echten Leben zu tun. Man findet diese Sendungen heutzutage auf jedem Programm. Man kann sie fast nicht vermeiden.

F Ich bin gar nicht einverstanden. Die Zuschauer finden diese Shows spannend. Meine Eltern haben mir neulich gesagt, dass ich süchtig bin. Meiner Meinung nach geht es um einen Wettbewerb, wo die Leute viel Geld verdienen wollen oder berühmt werden. Man will nur seinen Traum erfüllen, z.B. ein berühmter Sänger werden und ab und zu haben diese Leute sogar Talent. Es sind meistens normale Menschen, die an den Shows teilnehmen. Ich stimme für die Kandidaten, die ich am meisten mag.

M Spinnst du? Weißt du nicht, dass alles inszeniert ist? Was ich schrecklich finde, ist dass die Kandidaten manchmal schockierende und peinliche Aktivitäten unternehmen. Ich bin der Meinung, dass Reality TV einen schlechten Einfluss auf die Jugendlichen ausübt. Einige Teenager glauben, dass es sich nicht lohnt in der Schule fleißig zu arbeiten, weil sie wegen solcher Sendungen schnell reich werden können. Es gibt viele Leute, die etwas für die Gesellschaft leisten und ich möchte lieber einen Dokumentarfilm darüber sehen.

F Was ich am besten finde, ist, dass ich das Leben von anderen Menschen beobachten kann und wie sie miteinander umgehen. Man kann viel über die Menschlichkeit lernen. Es gibt mir die Hoffnung, dass ich eines Tages mein Leben ändern kann. Vielleicht sollte ich mich für die nächste Serie bewerben.

Questions

1 Why did Florian enjoy watching the reality TV show? (2)
2 What does Melanie think about reality TV? (2)
3 Why does she think it is difficult to avoid reality TV programmes? (1)
4 What does Florian say the programmes are about? (2)
5 What does Melanie find terrible about such shows? (1)
6 What does Melanie say about reality TV and young people? (3)
7 What would Melanie rather watch? (1)
8 What does Florian find interesting about the reality TV shows? (2)

⚙ ACTIVITY: Big Brother contestants

Some Big Brother contestants give their opinions of being on the show. What did they like/dislike about the experience?

 Es hat mir meistens viel Spaß gemacht. Ich habe mich mit den anderen Hausbewohnern gut verstanden. Ich war nur ab und zu ein bisschen einsam. – **Jonas**

 Wir mussten alles selber kochen und das fand ich sehr schwierig. Zum Glück konnte ich jeden Morgen ausschlafen. Das war Luxus! – **Philipp**

 Ich fand es prima, dass mich meine Familie jeden Abend im Fernsehen sehen konnte. Ich habe aber meine Freunde vermisst und das hat mir nicht so gut gefallen. – **Alina**

▶ VIDEO LINK

Head to www. brightredbooks.net/ N5German to watch some great clips on this topic.

➕ DON'T FORGET

Try to pick out phrases you could use in a talking or writing assessment to discuss the good and bad points about watching TV and reality TV in particular.

✓ ONLINE TEST

Try the online test about Reality TV at www. brightredbooks.net/ N5German

ⓘ THINGS TO DO AND THINK ABOUT

When using discursive language it is a good idea to show both sides of an argument:
- auf der einen Seite ... on the one hand
- auf der anderen Seite ... on the other hand

TECHNOLOGY – DIE TECHNOLOGIE

BIST DU OFT AM COMPUTER? – DO YOU SPEND A LOT OF TIME ON THE COMPUTER?

Fortunately, many words to do with computers are the same in German as in English:

> **EXAMPLE:**
>
> der Computer   das Internet

Here is a good structure for an essay or talk on computers:

- how often you use a computer
- what you use the computer for
- the dangers of the internet
- how to stay safe

Technology, particularly computers, plays an important role in most people's daily lives. You should be able to say how often you use your computer and what you use your computer for:

Ich benutze meinen Computer oft/manchmal/jeden Tag.

- Ich besuche Chatrooms. – I visit chatrooms.
- Ich lade Fotos hoch. – I upload photos.
- Ich spiele Computerspiele. – I play computer games.
- Ich schreibe E-mails. – I write e-mails.
- Ich lade Musik herunter. – I download music.
- Ich mache meine Hausaufgaben. – I do homework.
- Ich mache Einkäufe online. – I shop online.
- Ich schaue lustige Videos an. – I watch funny videos.
- Ich lese die Profile von meinen Freunden. – I read my friends' profiles.
- Ich mache Forschung für einen Schulprojekt. – I do research for a school project.
- Ich surfe im Internet. – I surf the internet.

⚙ ACTIVITY   The dangers of the internet

Read the following leaflet designed for school pupils outlining the dangers of the internet and what precautions can be taken.

Translate the bullet points into English.

> Die Sicherheit im Internet ist ein Problem. Es gibt viele Risiken. Man muss vorsichtig sein.
>
> - Die Informationen sind nicht immer korrekt, wie zum Beispiel auf Wikipedia.
> - Es gibt viele Computerviren. Die Viren machen den Computer kaputt.
> - Das Internet ist ein Forum für Gewalt und Pornographie.
> - Cybermobbing ist ein großes Problem.
> - Es gibt Leute, die ein falsches Profil schreiben und böse Fotos hochladen.
> - Es gibt viele Hacker.
> - Datenklau ist ein Problem.
> - Pädophile benutzen das Internet. Sie geben einen falschen Namen und ein falsches Alter an und chatten wie einen Freund.
>
> **Sicherheitstipps**
>
> - Man sollte sein Profil nur für Familie und Freunde schreiben.
> - Man sollte einen Spitznamen in Chatrooms benutzen.
> - Man sollte keine doofen Fotos hochladen.
> - Man sollte Kontaktdaten nicht herausgeben, besonders die Adresse und die Telefonnummer.

MEIN HANDY – MY MOBILE PHONE

 ## ACTIVITY: Survey about mobile phones

The pupils of Class 10a at the Stormanschule in Ahrensburg were asked to fill in a short questionnaire about mobile phones. Here are the results.

FRAGE 1: WIE OFT BENUTZT DU DEIN HANDY?	
Ich benutze ständig mein Handy	80%
Ich benutze manchmal mein Handy	14%
Ich benutze mein Handy sehr wenig	5%
Ich benutze nie mein Handy	1%

Explain the following percentages in English:

a 5% **b** 80% **c** 1%

FRAGE 2: WOFÜR BENUTZT DU DAS HANDY AM MEISTEN?	
Ich rufe Freunde an	27%
Ich lade Fotos hoch	12%
Ich lade Ringtöne herunter	20%
Ich spiele Computerspiele	6%
Ich surfe im Internet	8%
Ich simse	23%
Ich informiere mich	4%

Explain the following percentages in English:

a 20% **b** 27% **c** 12% **d** 23% **e** 4%

 ## ACTIVITY: Das Handy: pro oder kontra?

Are the following statements for or against mobile phones? Put a tick or a cross beside each one. Now translate the sentences into English.

1 Es ist gut für die Sicherheit, zum Beispiel wenn man in den Bergen wandert.
2 Das Handy ist wie eine Droge.
3 Meine Eltern können mich immer erreichen.
4 Einige Leute benutzen das Handy beim Autofahren. Das ist gefährlich.
5 Ein Handy klingelt im Klassenzimmer. Es stört den Unterricht.
6 Es ist wichtig in einem Notfall, zum Beispiel, wenn das Auto eine Panne auf der Autobahn hat.
7 Einige Leute simsen ständig.
8 Die Rechnung ist immer sehr hoch.
9 Ein Handy ist mehr als ein Telefon. Mein Handy ist Fernseher, Kamera und Organiser.
10 Einige Leute sprechen sehr laut am Handy.
11 Die Antennenmasten sind schrecklich.
12 Wenn der Bus nicht kommt, kann ich meine Eltern schnell anrufen.

 ## THINGS TO DO AND THINK ABOUT

Another way of using discursive language in your writing or talk is to consider the advantages and disadvantages of a topic:

- der Vorteil – the advantage
- der Nachteil – the disadvantage

EXAMPLE

Der Vorteil meines Handys ist, dass ich meine Freunde und meine Eltern jederzeit erreichen kann. Der Nachteil ist, dass die Rechnung oft sehr hoch ist.

 ### DON'T FORGET

Note how in German the letters 'er' are added to the adjective for comparisons, e.g. *schnell* = fast, *schneller* = faster, *praktisch* = practical, *praktischer* = more practical.

ONLINE

Check out the additional activities on Facebook and on mobile phones at www.brightredbooks.net/N5German

 ### VIDEO LINK

Check out the clip 'Ein Leben OHNE Handy' at www.brightredbooks.net/N5German

 ### ONLINE TEST

Take the online test about technology at www.brightredbooks.net/N5German

DOING SPORT – SPORT TREIBEN

Sport is popular among German teenagers. You will learn to say whether you are sporty or not as well as what sports you do and where and when you do them. Here are some ideas to help you prepare for a writing task or assessment.

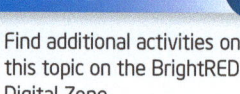

ONLINE

Find additional activities on this topic on the BrightRED Digital Zone.

BIST DU SPORTLICH? – ARE YOU SPORTY?

- Ich bin sehr sportlich. Sport ist mein Leben. – I am very sporty. Sport is my life.
- Ich bin echt/wirklich sportlich. – I am really sporty.
- Ich bin ganz/ziemlich sportlich. – I am quite sporty.
- Ich bin nicht sportlich. Ich bin faul. – I am not sporty. I am lazy.
- Ich sehe Sport lieber im Fernsehen. – I prefer watching sport on TV.
- Ich bin ein Stubenhocker. – I am a couch potato.
- Ich bin eine Sportskanone. – I am sport-mad.

For the majority of ball sports, German uses the same word as in English, for example Volleyball, Basketball, Tennis and so on.

Here are some of the harder sports to recognise:

- Fechten – fencing
- Turnen – gymnastics
- Laufen – running
- Gewichte heben – weightlifting
- Federball – badminton

- Segeln – sailing
- Rudern – rowing
- Radfahren – cycling
- Reiten – horseriding
- Wandern – hillwalking
- Kegeln – bowling

- Bogenschießen – archery
- Leichtathletik – athletics
- Eislaufen – ice-skating
- Klettern – climbing
- Angeln – fishing

Give your opinion on the sports listed above. Use the phrases and adjectives listed below to help you.

- lustig – fun
- schnell – fast
- spannend – exciting
- entspannend – relaxing

- anstrengend – tiring
- interessant – interesting
- einfach – easy
- schwierig – difficult

- teuer – expensive
- gefährlich – dangerous
- langweilig – boring
- es macht Spaß – it is fun

EXAMPLE:

Wie findest du Fechten? What do you think about fencing?

This is how you would give your opinion:

Ich finde Fechten gefährlich. = I find fencing dangerous.

Meiner Meinung nach ist Fechten gefährlich. = In my opinion, fencing is dangerous.

⚙ ACTIVITY Warum treibt man Sport? – Why do people do sport?

Many German teenagers spend their afternoons doing sport. Here are some of the reasons they give for doing the various sports. Translate the reasons into English.

1. Es ist gesund.
2. Man sieht jünger aus.
3. Es macht Spaß.
4. Man fühlt sich fit und wohl.
5. Man ist nicht so oft krank.
6. Man hat mehr Ausdauer und Energie.
7. Man bekommt eine schlanke Figur.
8. Man ist selbstsicherer.
9. Man kann neue Freunde kennen lernen.
10. Es ist eine Pause von dem Stress des Alltags.
11. Es ist gesellig.
12. Man lernt Teamgeist.

When talking about what sports you do, three main verbs are used: *spielen* = to play, *gehen* = to go and *machen* = to do.

ACTIVITY: Fill in the blanks

Complete each sentence by filling in the correct verb: *spiele, gehe* or *mache*:

1 Ich _____ Federball.
2 Ich _____ kegeln.
3 Ich _____ wandern.
4 Ich _____ Bogenschießen.

5 Ich _____ segeln.
6 Ich _____ Fechten.
7 Ich _____ Handball.
8 Ich _____ Gewichte heben.

ACTIVITY: When and how often do you do sport?

You should also be able to say when and how often you do sport. When or how often do these people do sport?

1 am Samstagmorgen
2 am Freitagabend
3 jeden Tag
4 zweimal in der Woche

5 am Wochenende
6 in den Ferien
7 am Donnerstagnachmittag
8 nach der Schule

9 einmal in der Woche
10 jeden Mittwoch

ACTIVITY: Who do you play with?

You could also say who you play with. Fill in the correct word for 'my': *meinem* = for males, *meiner* = for females, *meinen* = plural.

1 mit _____ Vater
2 mit _____ Schwester
3 mit _____ Freunden

4 mit _____ Kusine
5 mit _____ Bruder
6 mit _____ Eltern

7 mit _____ Freund
8 mit _____ Mutter

ACTIVITY: Where do you play?

You could also say where you do the sport. What do these words mean?

1 am Meer
2 in der Sporthalle
3 im Jugendzentrum
4 auf dem Land
5 am Sportplatz
6 im Hallenbad
7 am See
8 im Fitnessstudio

When you put all the information together, you need to observe the word-order rule: 1 when; 2 with whom; 3 where.

EXAMPLE

Ich spiele Tennis am Sonntag mit meiner Mutter am Sportplatz.

ACTIVITY: Building sentences

Try to build these sentences in German:

1 I go horse-riding on a Saturday with my friends in the countryside.
2 I go swimming on a Thursday with my dad at the sports centre.
3 I go sailing at the weekend with my parents at the lake.

THINGS TO DO AND THINK ABOUT

You could also adapt the following sentences to give more information about the sports that you enjoy doing.

- Ich bin Mitglied der Volleyballmannschaft in der Schule. – I am a member of the volleyball team at school.
- Wir haben die letzten drei Spiele gewonnen. – We have won the last three matches.
- Ich habe viele Preise/Pokale/Medaillen gewonnen. – I have won lots of prizes/trophies/medals.

HEALTH – DIE GESUNDHEIT

ISST DU GESUND? – DO YOU EAT HEALTHILY?

Health is a very important topic for Germans. In this section, you will revise words for healthy and unhealthy foods as well as learn how to discuss healthy and unhealthy eating habits.

⚙ ACTIVITY: Healthy and unhealthy food

Copy down the following two headings:

gesundes Essen = healthy food   ungesundes Essen = unhealthy food

Decide which heading each of these foods should go under:

Seelachs   Vollkornbrot   Torte   Pommes   Obst   Süßigkeiten   Käse   Gulasch   Chips

Reis   Bratkartoffeln   Frikadellen   Gemüse   Schinken   Schaschlik   Hähnchen

⚙ ACTIVITY: Eating habits 1

Do the following people have healthy eating habits or not? Write down *ja* = yes or *nein* = no. Then translate the sentences into English.

1   Ich esse nichts zum Frühstück.
2   Ich esse einen Apfel in der Pause.
3   Ich nasche sehr gern. Ich bin eine Naschkatze.
4   Zum Mittagessen esse ich ein Schinkenbrot mit Salat.
5   Wenn ich Hunger habe, esse ich eine Packung Chips.
6   Ich trinke acht Gläser Wasser pro Tag.
7   Ich esse viel Tiefkühlkost.
8   Ich vermeide fettiges Essen.
9   Zum Frühstück esse ich eine Tafel Schokolade.
10 Wenn ich Hunger habe, esse ich eine Banane.
11 Ich kaufe biologisches Essen.
12 Zum Abendessen esse ich Fisch mit Reis.
13 Ich esse Bonbons in der Pause.
14 Ich esse nie zwischen den Mahlzeiten.
15 Ich trinke nur Limonade oder Cola.
16 Ich esse fünf Portionen Obst und Gemüse pro Tag.
17 Zum Abendessen esse ich Bratwurst mit Bratkartoffeln.
18 Zum Mittagessen esse ich einen Hamburger mit Pommes.
19 Ich esse meistens Vollkornbrot.
20 Ich gehe oft zum Schnellimbiss.

ACTIVITY: Das Frühstück ist wichtig

While out shopping in Germany, you pick up two information leaflets in a Reformhaus (health shop). The first offers advice about the importance of eating breakfast.

Frühstück hält fit und schlank

Das Frühstück ist für viele Menschen ein kulinarisches Fest – doch leider meist nur am Wochenende. In der Woche haben die meisten Leute keine Zeit zum frühstücken. Nur circa jeder Dritte isst jeden Morgen Frühstück.

Das Frühstück ist laut Experten die wichtigste Mahlzeit des Tages. Warum? Ganz einfach: Über Nacht hat unser Körper Ruhepause. Der Körper muss sich regenerieren. Doch auch während der Regenerationsphase verbrauchen wir Energie. Deshalb sind unsere Reserven am Morgen aufgebraucht und wir benötigen neue Energie, um die optimale Leistung für den Tag erbringen zu können.

Richtig frühstücken hält fit

Beim Frühstück sollte man die richtigen Nahrungsmittel essen. Es ist wichtig für die Leistungsfähigkeit und die schlanke Figur. Man sollte Kohlenhydrate (in Vollkornprodukten und Müsli enthalten) mit Ballaststoffen (Obst und Gemüse) und eiweißreichen Lebensmitteln (Schinken, Käse oder Milch) kombinieren: Dieser Mix hilft unserem Gedächtnis und steigert die Konzentrationsfähigkeit. Zucker sollte man vermeiden, da diese sich negativ auf den Blutzuckerspiegel auswirken – Leistungsabfall und Heißhunger können die Folge sein.

1 How many Germans have breakfast? (1)
2 What do experts say about breakfast? (1)
3 Why does the body need energy at night? (1)
4 Why is it so important to eat the right food for breakfast? (2)
5 What would be suitable foods to eat at breakfast? (6)
6 What negative effect can sugar have? (2)

The second leaflet gives more general advice about having a healthy diet.

Summarise the six tips in English.

Wie ernährt man sich gesund?

Hier ein paar Tipps, wie du dich gesund und ausgewogen ernähren kannst:

1 Nehmen Sie über den Tag verteilt fünf Mahlzeiten zu sich, dann entwickeln Sie keinen Heißhunger.

2 Nehmen Sie „5 am Tag": Toll wäre es, wenn Sie fünfmal am Tag Obst und Gemüse essen würden, entweder als Zwischenmahlzeit oder zu den Hauptmahlzeiten. Das bringt reichlich Vitamine und Mineralstoffe.

3 Viel trinken! Über den Tag verteilt sollten Sie mindestens 1,5 Liter Flüssigkeit zu sich nehmen, am besten Wasser oder verdünnte Fruchtsäfte (keine Limonaden oder Energy-Drinks).

4 Milch und Milchprodukte sind generell gesund, da sie viel Calcium enthalten. Sie sollten jedoch darauf achten, dass die Produkte nicht zu sehr gesüßt und möglichst aus fettarmer Milch hergestellt sind.

5 Fleisch und Wurst sollten nur in geringen Mengen verzehrt werden. Fisch dagegen ist sehr gesund und sollte mindestens einmal in der Woche auf dem Speiseplan stehen.

6 Versuchen Sie, nicht zu viel Süßes zu essen. Ein Schokoriegel ist mal erlaubt, sollte aber nicht bei richtigem Hunger eine Mahlzeit ersetzen. Generell enthalten Gummibärchen deutlich weniger Fett als Schokolade.

THINGS TO DO AND THINK ABOUT

ONLINE TEST

Test yourself on this topic at www.brightredbooks.net/ N5German

Write a paragraph about your eating and drinking habits. Try to use some of the following phrases:

- Ich bin gesund/ungesund
- Ich esse viel ...
- Ich esse wenig ...
- Ich esse gern ... und ich esse nicht gern ...
- Mein Lieblingsessen ist ...
- Zum Frühstuck esse ich ...
- In der Pause esse ich ...
- Wenn ich Hunger habe, esse ich ...
- Ich trinke meistens ...
- Mein Lieblingsgetränk ist ...

DO YOU HAVE A HEALTHY LIFESTYLE? – LEBST DU GESUND?

In this section, you will learn how to discuss whether you have a healthy lifestyle or not and will be able to give examples.

⚙ ACTIVITY: Lifestyle questionnaire

You find a questionnaire in a German magazine about lifestyles and decide to complete it. Copy out the sentence that is the most true about your lifestyle for each section:

Wie gesund ist dein Leben?

1. Ich gehe zu Fuß zur Schule.

   Ich fahre mit dem Auto zur Schule.

2. Ich sehe stundenlang fern jeden Abend.

   Ich sehe eine Stunde fern jeden Abend.

3. Ich benutze mein Handy ab und zu.

   Ich bin ständig am Handy.

4. Ich treibe viel Sport.

   Ich treibe wenig Sport.

5. Ich benutze die Treppe im Kaufhaus.

   Ich benutze den Fahrstuhl im Kaufhaus.

6. Ich entspanne mich jeden Tag.

   Ich bin immer gestresst.

7. Ich putze mir die Zähne zweimal in der Woche.

   Ich putze mir die Zähne zweimal am Tag.

8. Ich dusche mich oft.

   Ich dusche mich selten.

9. Ich schlafe sechs Stunden jede Nacht.

   Ich schlafe acht Stunden jede Nacht.

10. Ich habe viele Freunde.

    Ich habe keine Freunde.

11. Ich rauche viel.
    Es ist gesellig.

    Ich rauche nie.
    Es ist ekelhaft.

12. Ich verbringe viel Zeit draussen an der frischen Luft.

    Ich verbringe wenig Zeit draussen an der frischen Luft.

⚙ ACTIVITY: Leading a healthy lifestyle

Some German teenagers discuss whether they can manage to lead a healthy lifestyle or not:

Read the following statements in German and complete the task below:

Thomas Ich vermeide zu viel Fett.

Lisa Ich esse jede Menge Gemüse.

Leon Wenn ich joggen gehe, kann ich von meinen Sorgen abschalten.

Paul Ich finde es wichtig, gesund zu leben.

Christina Ich gehe zu einem Yoga-Kurs, weil es gut für meine Seele ist.

Lara Ich denke, dass frisches Obst langweilig ist.

Lukas Ich bin Schokoladensüchtig. Je hungriger ich werde, umso mehr esse ich.

Felix Ich halte mich eher bei Fastfood zurück.

Julia Ich mache Spaziergänge mit meinem Hund.

Moritz Ich passe auf, was ich esse.

Florian Ich habe keine Zeit, Sport zu treiben.

Lena Das Golfspielen hilft mir mich zu entspannen und zu relaxen.

Michael Ich mache so viel Sport wie möglich.

Gabi Zum Frühstück esse ich einen Joghurt mit wenig Fett.

David Wenn ich hungrig bin, esse ich einen Apfel.

Luca Ich schwimme gern, weil es gut für meinen Körper ist.

Which teenager says ...?

1. I am addicted to chocolate. The more hungry I am, the more I eat.
2. Eating fruit is boring.
3. I tend to avoid fast food.
4. I avoid too much fat.
5. I do a yoga class because it is good for my mind.
6. I can forget my problems.

contd

7 I have no time to do sport.
8 I watch what I eat.
9 Swimming is good for my body.
10 I do as much sport as possible.
11 For breakfast I eat a diet yoghurt.

12 When I am hungry I eat an apple.
13 It is important to have a healthy life.
14 I go for walks with the dog.
15 I eat lots of vegetables.
16 Golf helps me unwind and relax.

 DON'T FORGET

In any writing task or talking assessment you do, it is important to use opinion phrases. You could start your sentence with: *Meiner Meinung nach* = in my opinion, or *Ich denke, dass ...* = I think that ... Look at examples in the texts.

ACTIVITY: Different lifestyles

Read the German texts and answer the questions that follow in English:

Oliver

Ich habe keine Zeit, Sport zu treiben. Als ich jünger war, habe ich viel Sport gemacht. Ich esse zu viel Fett und zu viele Süßigkeiten. Meine Mutter sagt, dass ich Fastfood vermeiden sollte und mehr Obst und Gemüse essen sollte. Nicht weit von meinem Haus hat ein Fitnessstudio aufgemacht. Wenn ich genug Energie habe, werde ich zum Training ins Fitnessstudio gehen.

1 Why does Oliver not exercise? (1)
2 When did he used to do sport? (1)
3 What kind of food does he eat too much of? (2)

4 What does his Mum advise him to do? (2)
5 Why might he now consider doing some exercise? (1)

Sabina

Meiner Meinung nach lebe ich gesund. Für mich ist gesunde Ernährung genauso wichtig wie Bewegung. Ich gehe zu einem Yoga-Kurs, um von meinen Sorgen abschalten zu können und um mich zu entspannen. Nach dem Yoga bin ich gelenkig und ich kann Dinge aus einer anderen Perspektive sehen. Ich bin nicht besonders scharf auf Fastfood und ich passe auf, was ich esse. Zum Beispiel esse ich einen Joghurt mit wenig Fett, wenn ich hungrig bin und ich habe immer Obst dabei.

1 What does Sabina say about herself in her opening statement? (1)
2 What does she say about healthy eating and exercise? (1)

3 Why does she do yoga classes? (2)
4 How does she feel after the class? (2)
5 What shows that she is a healthy eater? (2)

Hans

Ich denke, das Beste ist eine Kombination von richtiger Ernährung und Bewegung. Ich würde dir vorschlagen zu laufen und man sollte zu viel Fett vermeiden. Ich esse gesund. Ich esse viel Hähnchen und Fisch. Ich esse auch fünf Portionen Obst und Gemüse pro Tag. Es ist manchmal langweilig und schwierig, gesund zu essen. Bonbons und Schokolade vermisse ich schon! Aber die richtige Ernährung und die richtige Bewegung sind wichtig.

1 What advice is given by Hans in line one? (2)
2 What type of exercise does he recommend? (1)

3 What are we told to avoid? (1)
4 Give two details about his diet. (2)
5 Why can eating a healthy diet be difficult? (1)

 ONLINE TEST

Try the online test about lifestyles at www.brightredbooks.net/N5German

 ONLINE

For more activities on this topic, head to www.brightredbooks.net/N5German

 ## THINGS TO DO AND THINK ABOUT

Write a paragraph about your lifestyle and whether it is mainly healthy or unhealthy. You should use the exercises in this section for ideas. You could say what you should do:

Ich sollte + the infinitive (main verb)

Ich sollte mehr Obst essen. – I should eat more fruit.

Ich sollte zu Fuß zur Schule gehen. – I should walk to school.

TEENAGE ADDICTIONS – JUGENDSUCHT

KEY VOCABULARY

- rauchen – to smoke
- Ich rauche seit zwei Jahren. – I have been smoking for two years.
- Ich habe nie geraucht. – I have never smoked.
- die Zigaretten – cigarettes
- tödlich – deadly
- es ist schwierig aufzuhören – it is difficult to give up
- Ich trinke Alkohol. – I drink alcohol.
- betrunken – drunk
- Ich habe ein Alkoholproblem. – I have got an alcohol problem.
- Ich würde nie Drogen nehmen. – I would never take drugs.
- Ich bin drogensüchtig. – I am addicted to drugs.

ACTIVITY Opinions on smoking

What do these teenagers think about smoking?

1 Ich finde Rauchen gefährlich.
2 Ich finde Rauchen schrecklich.
3 Ich finde Rauchen ungesund.
4 Ich finde Rauchen ekelhaft.
5 Ich finde Rauchen ungesellig.
6 Ich finde Rauchen egoistisch.

ACTIVITY The physical effects of smoking

What are the most common physical effects of smoking?

1 Rauchen verursacht Lungenkrebs.
2 Rauchen verursacht Husten.
3 Rauchen verursacht Atembeschwerden.
4 Rauchen verursacht Herzkrankheit.
5 Rauchen verursacht eine gelbe Haut.
6 Rauchen verursacht Mundgeruch.

ACTIVITY For or against?

What reasons do these teenagers give for being for/against alcohol and/or smoking?

1 Ich rauche, weil es entspannend ist.
2 Ich rauche, weil ich schlechte Noten in der Schule habe.
3 Ich trinke keinen Alkohol, weil meine Freunde oft betrunken sind. Sie machen und sagen dummes Zeug.
4 Ich rauche nicht, weil es tödlich ist.
5 Ich rauche, weil es modisch ist.
6 Ich trinke Alkohol, um meine Sorgen zu vergessen.
7 Ich rauche, weil ich nicht aufhören kann.
8 Ich rauche, weil ich abnehmen muss.
9 Ich trinke Alkohol, um meine Hemmungen loszuwerden.
10 Ich rauche, weil es gesellig ist.
11 Ich rauche nicht, weil man schnell süchtig wird.
12 Ich trinke Alkohol, um zu der Clique zu gehören.
13 Wenn ich rauche, habe ich mehr Selbstvertrauen.
14 Ich rauche nicht, weil viele Leute an Lungenkrebs sterben.

Read the leaflets about smoking, alcohol and drugs and answer the questions in English.

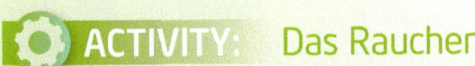 **ACTIVITY:** Das Rauchen

1. When do most people start smoking? (1)
2. Why do adults smoke? (1)
3. What is the biggest problem? (1)
4. Why is smoking so dangerous? Give two details. (2)
5. What is a common reason for smoking? (1)

Viele Menschen beginnen schon als Jugendliche mit dem Rauchen. Für Jugendliche sieht es schick aus und für Erwachsene ist es eher eine Stressbewältigung. Das größte Problem ist, dass man schnell süchtig wird und nicht mehr aufhören kann. Es gibt viele Gefahren. Das Rauchen ist eine Ursache für viele Krankheiten. In den schlimmsten Fällen kommt es zum Lungenkrebs. Das Rauchen kann tödlich sein. Im Tabak gibt es gefährliche Stoffe wie Nikotin und Teer. Was ist der Hauptgrund, warum so viele Jugendliche rauchen? Der Gruppendruck spielt eine große Rolle. Niemand will der Außenseiter sein. Man muss zu der Clique gehören.

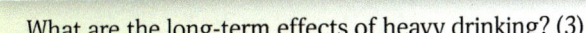 **ACTIVITY:** Der Alkoholismus

Sicherlich hast du schon von den Partys gehört, bei denen Übermassen Alkohol konsumiert werden. Starkes Trinken über längerer Zeit führt zu Leber-, Nieren- und Gehirnschädigungen. Der Genuss von Alkohol kann auch abhängig machen. Ist jemand erst einmal abhängig geworden und hat nichts zu trinken, führt das zu heftigem Zittern und Halluzinationen.

1. What are the long-term effects of heavy drinking? (3)
2. What happens if you become addicted and then try not to drink? (2)

 ONLINE

Head to the BrightRED Digital Zone for more activities on this topic.

 ACTIVITY: Jugendliche und Drogen

Unter Drogen versteht man Suchtmittel, die psychisch und meist körperlich süchtig machen. Für die meisten Jugendlichen bleibt das Drogennehmen eine Probierphase. Diese Phase beginnt während der Schulzeit und endet beim Eintritt in das Erwachsenenleben. Junge Leute wollen mit allem experimentieren. Das Hauptproblem ist, dass viele Jugendliche glauben, dass Drogen modisch sind. Sie ignorieren die Gefahren und genießen die Effekte. Mit Drogen chillt man und man kann die Nacht durchtanzen. Man hat weniger Hemmungen und es ist einfacher neue Menschen kennenzulernen, besonders wenn man schüchtern ist. Wenn der Konsum sich zur Gewohnheit entwickelt, ist es schwierig aufzuhören. Man wird so schnell süchtig. Drogen sind schlecht für das Herz und die Leber und man kann auch eine Blutkrankheit bekommen.

1. When does the drug-taking phase usually take place? (2)
2. What is the main problem? (2)
3. Mention three reasons why teenagers might take drugs. (3)
4. What damage can drugs do to your health? (3)

DON'T FORGET

Remember to use discursive language: *Ich bin für* = I am in favour of and *Ich bin gegen* = I am against.

ONLINE TEST

Test yourself on this vocabulary online at www.brightredbooks.net/N5German

 THINGS TO DO AND THINK ABOUT

Write a paragraph in German giving your opinion about smoking, alcohol and drugs.

MY HOME – MEIN ZUHAUSE

In this section, you will revise the key vocabulary relating to the house as well as learn how to describe your local area.

The following exercises test your knowledge of the key vocabulary. Remember to look up any words you are unsure of in the dictionary.

 **Buildings**

In what kind of building do these people live?

1 Ich wohne in einem Doppelhaus.
2 Ich wohne in einem Einfamilienhaus.
3 Ich wohne in einem Reihenhaus.
4 Ich wohne in einem Mehrfamilienhaus.

5 Ich wohne in einem Hochhaus.
6 Ich wohne in einer Wohnung.
7 Ich wohne in einem Bauernhaus.
8 Ich wohne in einem Wohnblock.

 **Where is your house?**

Where are the following houses located?

1 Mein Haus ist in einem Dorf.
2 Mein Haus ist in einer Stadt.
3 Mein Haus ist in den Bergen.
4 Mein Haus ist auf dem Land.
5 Mein Haus ist in einem Vorort.

6 Mein Haus ist am Meer.
7 Mein Haus ist in einer Großstadt.
8 Mein Haus ist an der Küste.
9 Mein Haus ist am Stadtrand.
10 Mein Haus ist in der Stadtmitte.

 **What is it like?**

What do these people say about their homes?

1 Mein Haus ist winzig aber hell.
2 Mein Haus ist dunkel und altmodisch.
3 Mein Haus ist riesig aber familienfreundlich.
4 Mein Haus ist schön und gut gepflegt.

5 Mein Haus ist großzügig und gemütlich.
6 Mein Haus ist ordentlich und bequem.
7 Mein Haus ist unordentlich und dreckig.
8 Mein Haus ist sauber und charmant.

 **Rooms**

Which rooms are on which floors?

1 Im Keller sind ein Spielraum und eine Waschküche.
2 Im Erdgeschoß gibt es ein Wohnzimmer, ein Esszimmer, eine Küche und eine Toilette.
3 Im ersten Stock sind drei Schlafzimmer, ein Badezimmer und ein Gästezimmer.
4 Im Dachboden gibt es ein Arbeitszimmer.

DEIN SCHLAFZIMMER BESCHREIBEN – DESCRIBING YOUR BEDROOM

Here is some useful vocabulary to help you describe your bedroom:

- Ich habe mein eigenes Zimmer. – I have my own room.
- Ich teile mein Zimmer mit meinem Bruder/meiner Schwester. – I share my room with my brother/sister.

contd

- Mein Zimmer ist meine Welt. – My room is my world.
- Mein Zimmer ist ordentlich/unordentlich/chaotisch. – My room is tidy/untidy/chaotic.
- Zeitschriften liegen auf dem Boden. – Magazines lie about the floor.
- Kleidung liegt auf dem Bett. – Clothes lie on top of the bed.
- Ich habe viele Poster an der Wand. – I have a lot of posters on the wall.
- Die Wände sind weiß. – The walls are white.
- Der Teppich ist grau. – The carpet is grey.
- Die Vorhänge sind blau. – The curtains are blue.

To give more precise information, you could use a compass point:

im Norden

im Westen

im Osten

im Süden

DEINE GEGEND BESCHREIBEN – DESCRIBING YOUR AREA

Wo wohnst du? – Where do you live? Ich wohne in + (town) in Schottland.
When combined: im Nordosten/im Südwesten

EXAMPLE

Ich wohne in Renfrew in Südwestschottland.

You could say which big town you live near:

EXAMPLE

Ich wohne in Renfrew in der Nähe von Glasgow/nicht weit von Glasgow.

The word for most German towns is the same in German and in English, for example Hamburg, Berlin, Frankfurt etc.

The towns that change are: Köln = Cologne, München = Munich, and the capital of Austria: Wien = Vienna.

You should also be aware of the region Bayern, which is Bavaria in English and is a region in the south of Germany.

Other important geographical areas you should know are:

der Schwarzwald = the Black Forest
der Bodensee = Lake Constance
die Ostsee = the Baltic Sea

der Rhein = the (river) Rhine
die Donau = the (river) Danube

 ONLINE TEST

Now try the online test on this topic at www.brightredbooks.net/N5German

 ONLINE

For more activities on this topic, head to www.brightredbooks.net/N5German

 ACTIVITY: Meine Gegend

Where are these towns situated?

1 Die Stadt liegt an der Grenze mit Frankreich.
2 Die Stadt liegt an der Ostküste.
3 Meine Stadt liegt im Schwarzwald.
4 Meine Stadt liegt am Rhein.
5 Meine Stadt ist die Hauptstadt von Deutschland.
6 Meine Stadt liegt an der Ostsee.
7 Meine Stadt liegt in der Nähe vom Bodensee.
8 Meine Stadt liegt in Bayern.
9 Meine Stadt liegt an der Donau.
10 Meine Stadt ist Wien, die Hauptstadt von Österreich.

 DON'T FORGET

Note that in German a full stop is used with numbers, instead of a comma as in English. For example, 4.000 = 4,000.

 ## THINGS TO DO AND THINK ABOUT

Using the phrases you have been learning in this section, write a paragraph about where you live and describe your town/village, house and bedroom.

MY TOWN – MEINE STADT

DESCRIBING YOUR LOCAL AREA

You could say how many inhabitants are in the town.

You use the word *ungefähr* or *etwa* before a number to mean 'about' when you are not sure of the exact number.

> **EXAMPLE**
>
> Es gibt ungefähr vier tausend Einwohner. – There are about 4,000 inhabitants.

It would be useful to be able to describe your local area. Can you think of any adjectives that you could use?

ACTIVITY: Adjectives

Here are a few adjectives to start you off. Look up any words you are not familiar with in the dictionary, then put the adjectives under the headings positive/negative:

schön langweilig sauber ruhig schmutzig uralt häßlich laut deprimierend

lebendig historisch hübsch verschmutzt wunderbar umweltfreundlich

gut gepflegt sicher gefährlich

You could say what the town is famous for:

> **EXAMPLE:**
>
> Die Stadt ist für ... bekannt.

ACTIVITY: Why are these towns famous?

1 Meine Stadt ist für die Wanderwege bekannt.
2 Meine Stadt ist für die Fußballmannschaft bekannt.
3 Meine Stadt ist für die Kirchen bekannt.
4 Meine Stadt ist für das Musikfest bekannt.
5 Meine Stadt ist für die alten Häuser bekannt.
6 Meine Stadt ist für die Sehenswürdigkeiten bekannt.
7 Meine Stadt ist für das Einkaufszentrum bekannt.
8 Meine Stadt ist für Wildwasserfahren bekannt.
9 Meine Stadt ist für die Bergen bekannt.
10 Meine Stadt ist für den Fernsehturm bekannt.

 **ACTIVITY:** Where I live

Read the German texts and complete the tasks:

Matthias

Ich wohne in einem hübschen Dorf an der Küste. Im Sommer kommen viele Touristen aus aller Welt um mein Dorf zu besuchen. Man kann einen schönen Spaziergang am Strand entlang machen oder man kann einen Stadtbummel machen, um sich die historischen Gebäude anzuschauen. Für diejenige, die gern Wassersport treiben, bietet mein Dorf eine gute Auswahl von Aktivitäten. Man kann segeln oder windsurfen gehen. Angeln ist auch eine Möglichkeit. Man kann sogar eine Bootsfahrt machen und eine kleine Insel besichtigen.

Kerstin

Ich wohne in einer Großstadt. Obwohl die Stadt sehr groß ist, finde ich die Stadt ganz schön. Es gibt viele Parks, die gut gepflegt sind mit vielen Bäumen und Blumenbeeten. Es gibt viel zu tun und zu sehen. Man kann eine Tageskarte kaufen und mit der U-Bahn herumfahren und sich die Sehenswürdigkeiten anschauen. Ich würde die Stadtrundfahrt mit dem Bus empfehlen. Es ist viel einfacher und bequemer. Die Stadt bietet viele Unterhaltungsmöglichkeiten: Museen, Kunstgalerien, Kinos, Kegelbahnen usw. Es gibt was für jeden Geschmack. Was Unterkunft betrifft, kann man etwas zu jedem Preis finden, vom Luxushotel zu einem Campingplatz oder einer Jugendherberge.

1   Where do Matthias and Kerstin live?
2   What is there for tourists to do in their home areas?

 **ACTIVITY:** Düsseldorf

You pick up a tourist information leaflet about the town of Düsseldorf. Translate the following sentences into English.

1   Düsseldorf ist ein ehemaliges Fischerdorf, das an dem Fluss Düssel liegt.
2   Der Flughafen in Düsseldorf ist der drittgrößte Flughafen Deutschlands.
3   Von allen großen europäischen Metropolen erreichen Sie Düsseldorf in nur einer Flugstunde.
4   Düsseldorf ist Gastgeber für über 40 internationale Messen im Jahr.
5   Diese Stadt pulsiert mit 260 Lokalen, Kneipen, Brauhäusern und Cafés.
6   Die Altstadt ist bildschön mit engen Gassen mit Kopfsteinpflaster.
7   Man kann an der Rheinuferpromenade spazieren.
8   Düsseldorf ist eine Modestadt. Entlang der Königsallee präsentieren sich internationale Luxusmarken wie Gucci, Burberry und Chanel.
9   Ob zu Fuß, per Bus, oder per Schiff, bieten geführte Stadtbesichtigungen einen ersten Überblick über die Stadt und sind ein informatives wie unterhaltsames Erlebnis.
10 Grün ist eine dominante Farbe in Düsseldorf. Knapp ein Fünftel der Grundfläche der Stadt sind Grün- und Waldflächen. Man nennt Düsseldorf die Gartenstadt.

 ## THINGS TO DO AND THINK ABOUT

You can improve sentences by adding in a qualifier.

> **EXAMPLE**
>
> Meine Stadt ist sehr sauber und ganz lebenidg.
> Meine Stadt ist wirklich historisch und ziemlich hubsch.

Translate the two Sentences into English then try to build your own German sentence about your town.

A TOURIST TOWN – EINE TOURISTENSTADT

In this section, you will learn how to describe why tourists might come to your home area. We will revise the words for different places in town and the rules for adjective endings.

⚙ ACTIVITY: Home towns

Listen to the following texts online and fill in the blanks using the words in the box below.

Read the text first to get the gist of what it is about and try to predict what you are going to hear.

Ich wohne in Renfrew in Schottland. Die Stadt liegt im _____ in der Nähe von Glasgow. Ich finde meine Stadt _____ und historisch, aber ein bißchen _____.

> lebendig   schmutzig   Südwesten

Ich wohne in Alloway. Es ist ein Dorf _____. Das Dorf ist schön, _____ und sauber. Das Dorf ist für den Dichter Robert Burns _____.

> ruhig   bekannt   an der Küste

Ich wohne in Braemar nicht weit von den _____. Die Stadt liegt im _____. Die Stadt ist klein, _____ und wunderbar. Die Stadt ist für _____ bekannt.

> hübsch   Bergen   das Schloss   Nordosten

DER TOURISMUS IN DEINER HEIMATSTADT – TOURISM IN YOUR HOME AREA

Can you think of what tourists visiting your home area might like to do?

⚙ ACTIVITY:

Can you remember the English words for these buildings that you might find in your town? Look up the words you don't know in the dictionary.

- das Krankenhaus
- die Kirche
- der Bahnhof
- die Bibliothek
- das Hallenbad

- der Dom
- der Hafen
- der Tierpark
- das Freibad
- das Kino

- das Schloss
- das Rathaus
- die Fußgängerzone

Grammar

Es gibt ... – There is/are ...

The word for 'a' changes depending on whether the noun is masculine (*der*), feminine (*die*) or neuter (*das*):

contd

EXAMPLE

der Bahn of	Es gibt **einen** Bahnhof.
die Bibliothek	Es gibt **eine** Bibliothek.
das Freibad	Es gibt **ein** Freibad.

To make the sentence negative, you put a 'k' before the word for 'a': *keinen/keine/kein*:

EXAMPLE

Es gibt keinen Bahnhof, keine Bibliothek und kein Freibad. – There is no station, no library and no outdoor pool.

Plurals of German nouns need to be learned by heart as there are so many variations. You can check the plural form in the dictionary.

If you add an adjective, then it also has to agree with the noun:

EXAMPLE

Es gibt einen groß**en** Bahnhof.   Es gibt ein schön**es** Freibad.

Es gibt eine modern**e** Bibliothek.

ACTIVITY: Adjectives

Write out these sentences filling in the correct adjective ending.

1. Es gibt eine hübsch____ Kirche.
2. Es gibt einen neu____ Hafen.
3. Es gibt ein interessant____ Rathaus.
4. Es gibt einen toll____ Tierpark.
5. Es gibt ein alt____ Schloss.

Was kann man machen?

Man kann ...

When using this phrase, the main verb goes to the end of the sentence:

EXAMPLE

Man kann einkaufen **gehen**.	You can go shopping.
Man kann Wildwasser **fahren**.	You can go white-water rafting.
Man kann eine Bootsfahrt **machen**.	You can go on a boat trip.

It is good to use subordinating conjunctions in your writing and performance tasks. Here are some ideas.

Note that *wo* = where sends the verb to the end of the sentence.

- Es gibt einen tollen Park, wo man schön spazieren kann. – There is a great park where you can go for a nice walk.
- Es gibt eine schöne Fußgängerzone, wo man gut einkaufen kann. – There is a nice pedestrian area where you can do some good shopping.
- Es gibt ein modernes Kino, wo man die neuesten Filme sehen kann. – There is a modern cinema where you can see the latest films.

THINGS TO DO AND THINK ABOUT

Write a paragraph about a tourist town or village near where you live. You should make use of the phrases and grammar points above to express your own ideas.

DON'T FORGET

The word *Möglichkeiten* = facilities is used a lot in German, e.g. *Sportmöglichkeiten* = sports facilities, *Einkaufsmöglichkeiten* = shopping facilities.

ONLINE TEST

Try out the online test to revise the vocabulary and grammar from this section at www.brightredbooks.net/ N5German

ONLINE

For more activities on this topic, head to www. brightredbooks.net/ N5German

TOWN AND COUNTRY – STADT UND LAND

In this section, we will compare life in a town to life in the country.

DAS LEBEN IN DER STADT UND AUF DEM LAND – TOWN AND COUNTRY LIFE

Can you think of the main differences between the two ways of life?

 **ACTIVITY** Advantages and disadvantages

Translate the following phrases:

1 What are the advantages of living in the town?
   a   Es gibt viel für junge Leute.
   b   Das Nachtleben ist ausgezeichnet.
   c   Es ist lebendig.
   d   Es ist viel los.
   e   Es gibt viele Einkaufsmöglichkeiten und Unterhaltungsmöglichkeiten.
   f   Man hat eine gute Auswahl von Geschäften und Lokalen.
   g   Die Verkehrsmittel sind toll.
   h   Die Geschäfte sind vierundzwanzig Stunden geöffnet.

2 What are the disadvantages of living in the town?
   a   Es gibt zu viel Verkehr.
   b   Man kann nie einen Parkplatz finden.
   c   Die Luft ist verschmutzt.
   d   Die Straßen sind oft dreckig und es liegt viel Müll herum.
   e   Es ist gefährlich und man hat Angst nachts auszugehen.
   f   Es gibt zu viel Lärm.
   g   Das Leben ist stressig und hektisch.

3 What are the advantages of living in the country?
   a   Man hat viel Platz.
   b   Es gibt schöne Radwege und Wanderwege.
   c   Die Luft is frischer.
   d   Es ist viel ruhiger.
   e   Die Landschaft ist schön.
   f   Man wohnt mitten in der Natur.
   g   Es gibt wenig Kriminalität
   h   Jeder kennt sich.

4 What are the disadvantages of life in the country?
   a   Es gibt oft nur ein einziges Geschäft.
   b   Es gibt nichts zu tun.
   c   Man fühlt sich isoliert.
   d   Die Verkehrsmittel fahren nicht regelmäßig.
   e   Das Leben hier ist todlangweilig.
   f   Es gibt wenig Freizeitsmöglichkeiten.
   g   Meine Freunde wohnen weit weg.

 ACTIVITY Where I used to live

Read the following texts and answer the questions in English.

1 Where did each person used to live?
2 Mention two advantages of living there.
3 Mention two disadvantages of living there.

Thea

Als ich jünger war, wohnte ich auf dem Land. Wir sind umgezogen, weil mein Vater einen neuen Job gefunden hat. Ich mochte das Leben auf dem Land, weil jeder sich kannte und man viel Freiheit hatte. Man konnte draußen spielen, wenn das Wetter schön war, weil es viele Grünanlagen gab. Die Luft war frischer und es gab weniger Kriminalität. Das Problem war, dass die Verkehrsmittel nicht regelmäßig fuhren. Meine Freunde wohnten weit weg.

contd

Torsten

Als ich jünger war, wohnte ich in einer Großstadt. Ich fand das Leben dort spannend. Es gab viel zu tun. Man konnte ins Kino oder in die Eishalle gehen. Es gab eine gute Auswahl von Geschäften und Lokalen. Meine Mutter war oft krank. Sie fand die Luft zu verschmutzt in der Stadt. Für sie war das Leben zu stressig und hektisch. Letztes Jahr sind wir umgezogen.

GRAMMAR: DAS PRÄTERITUM – THE IMPERFECT TENSE

You need this tense to talk about the past. It is often referred to as the simple past, as it consists of just one word.

The simple past corresponds to a variety of English past tenses. For example, *ich spielte* can be translated into English as 'I played', 'I used to play', 'I was playing' and 'I did play'.

This is how you form the imperfect tense of regular verbs: spielen = to play

Remove the 'en' to get the stem, then add the following endings:

ich spiel**te**	I played/I used to play
du spiel**test**	you played/you used to play (one person you know)
er/sie/es spiel**te**	he/she/it played/used to play
wir spiel**ten**	we played/used to play
ihr spiel**tet**	you played/used to play (two or more people you know)
Sie spiel**ten**	you played/used to play (one or more strangers)
sie spiel**ten**	they played/used to play

Here are some verbs that change their stem. The endings they use are shown in the example verb:

gehen – to go	du ging**st**	wir ging**en**	Sie ging**en**
ich ging	er/sie/es ging	ihr ging**t**	sie ging**en**

INFINITIVE	PRESENT	IMPERFECT	ENGLISH
finden	ich finde	ich fand	I found
geben	ich gebe	ich gab	I gave
Note: es gibt/es gab = there is/was			
sein	ich bin	ich war	I was
Note: es ist/es war = it is/was			
können	ich kann	ich konnte	I could
mögen	ich mag	ich mochte	I liked
müssen	ich muss	ich musste	I had to
dürfen	ich darf	ich durfte	I was allowed to
haben	ich habe	ich hatte	I had
kennen	ich kenne	ich kannte	I knew
denken	ich denke	ich dachte	I thought

ONLINE TEST

The imperfect tense fits most topics, as you can talk about what you used to do. Test yourself online at www.brightredbooks.net/N5German

ONLINE

For more activities on this topic, head to www.brightredbooks.net/N5German

THINGS TO DO AND THINK ABOUT

In your performance and writing assessments, it is good to use discursive language where possible.

EXAMPLE

Ich wohne gern in der Stadt. Der Vorteil ist, dass es viel zu tun gibt. Der Nachteil ist, dass die Luft verschmutzt ist. – I like living in the town. The advantage is that there is lots to do. The disadvantage is that the air is polluted.

Note: dass sends the verb to the end of the sentence.

DON'T FORGET

Try always to give an opinion: **Meiner Meinung nach** ist das Leben in der Stadt zu stressig.

ENVIRONMENT – DIE UMWELT

In this section, you will learn to discuss the main environmental problems as well as what you, as an individual, can do to help.

 ACTIVITY: Was ist das größte Umweltproblem?

Let's start off by looking at the environmental problems that we are faced with. Read the phrases and translate them into English. Can you work out what they mean by making links to English phrases to do with environmental problems?

- die Luftverschmutzung
- die Wasserverschmutzung
- zu viel Müll
- die Lärmbelastung
- die Überbevölkerung
- die Verwüstung
- das Aussterben von Tierarten
- eine Erwärmung der Erdatmosphäre

- der Treibhauseffekt
- zu viel Verkehr und Staus auf der Autobahn
- Produkte mit zu viel Verpackung
- das Waldsterben
- das Ozonloch
- der saure Regen

ACTIVITY: Protecting the environment

What do these people do to help protect the environment?

1 Ich kaufe umweltfreundliche Produkte.
2 Ich recycle Altglas.
3 Ich trenne den Müll.
4 Ich fahre mit dem Rad.
5 Ich kompostiere den Abfall.
6 Ich nehme eine Öko-Tasche mit.
7 Ich fahre mit öffentlichen Verkehrsmitteln.

8 Ich kaufe Produkte mit wenig Verpackung.
9 Ich bringe meine alte Kleidung zu einer Sammelstelle.
10 Für die Schule kaufe ich mir Hefte aus Altpapier.
11 Ich werfe kein Papier auf die Straße.

ACTIVITY: Infinitives

This is a leaflet explaining what you should do to help protect the environment. Try to work out which infinitive belongs to each statement.

Umwelt in Gefahr

Was können wir machen, um die Umwelt zu schützen?

1 Man sollte _____ statt zu baden.

2 Man sollte mit öffentlichen Verkehrsmitteln _____.

3 Man sollte den Müll _____.

4 Man sollte den Fernseher _____.

5 Man sollte Papier und Altglas _____.

6 Man sollte den Geschirrspüler nur _____ , wenn er wirklich voll ist.

7 Man sollte den Abfall _____.

8 Man sollte umweltfreundliche Produkte _____.

recyceln   trennen   duschen   benutzen   kompostieren   fahren   kaufen   ausschalten

⚙ ACTIVITY: Magazine articles

You pick up a magazine about the environment in which you read three short articles on different topics. Answer the questions that follow in English.

The first article you read is about renewable energies.

1 How is most of our electricity produced? (3)
2 What are the disadvantages of using these types of energy? (3)
3 What types of energy would be better, and why? (5)

The second article describes what one group of people did to help protect the environment.

1 What event took place last Saturday? (1)
2 What was the first task? (1)
3 What shocked the writer? (2)
4 What did the group do next? (1)
5 What happened in the afternoon? (1)
6 What problem had not been anticipated? (1)

The third article explains why a group of animals is close to extinction.

1 Give two facts about the Sumatra elephant. (2)
2 Why is their living space under threat? (2)
3 What alarming statistic is given at the end of the text? (1)

Alternative Energiequellen

Jeden Tag verbrauchen wir Strom. Der größte Teil davon wird durch die Verbrennung von Kohle und Öl oder in Atomkraftwerken erzeugt. Die Vorräte von Kohle und Öl auf der Erde werden immer kleiner. Wenn man Erdöl verbrennt, um Elektrizität zu produzieren, setzt man Kohlendioxid frei. Und Atomkraft kann gefährlich sein. Deshalb will man mehr Energie aus der Natur nutzen. Wasser, Sonne und Wind verbrauchen sich nicht und sind umweltfreundlich.

Jeder kann was tun, um die Umwelt zu schützen

Letzten Samstag hatten wir einen Umwelt-Tag in unserer Schule. Wir haben uns um zehn Uhr auf dem Schulhof getroffen. Zuerst haben wir Abfall in der Stadtmitte gesucht und aufgesammelt. Ich fand es furchtbar, dass so viel Müll auf der Straße lag: Plastikflaschen, Verpackungen, Zigarettenkippen … Dann haben wir Öko-Taschen verteilt. Viele Leute haben sie genommen und sind damit im Supermarkt einkaufen gegangen. Am Nachmittag haben wir Broschüren mit Umwelt-Tipps verteilt: Fahrrad benutzen, Auto zu Hause lassen, Glas recyceln, duschen statt baden, und so weiter. Es gab nur ein Problem, dass wir nicht erwartet haben: Viele Leute haben die Broschüren einfach auf die Straße geworfen. Unglaublich!

Elefantenart vom Aussterben bedroht

Der Sumatra-Elefant ist vom Aussterben bedroht. In 30 Jahren könnte es die beeindruckenden Tiere nicht mehr geben, warnt der WWF. Der Sumatra-Elefant ist eine Art des asiatischen Elefanten und das größte Landtier Indonesiens. Die Tiere können mehr als sechs Meter lang und über drei Meter groß werden. Bei einer solchen Größe brauchen sie natürlich auch ausreichend Lebensraum. Der Lebensraum der Elefanten wird von Tag zu Tag wegen Abholzung kleiner. Für die Holzgewinnung und um Äcker anzulegen, werden immer mehr indonesische Wälder gerodet. Damit wird die Heimat der Sumatra-Elefanten vernichtet – und damit ihre Zukunft. Noch maximal 2800 Elefanten gibt es in Indonesien. Das sind halb so viele wie vor 30 Jahren.

 ONLINE TEST

Try the online test at www. brightredbooks.net/N5German to revise vocabulary on the environment and to learn vocabulary on natural disasters.

 DON'T FORGET

Start your sentence with ich sollte to express what you should do.

ⓘ THINGS TO DO AND THINK ABOUT

Write a short essay about the environment. You could mention:

- what you consider to be the biggest environmental problems
- what you do to protect the environment
- what you could do or what you intend to do in the future.

 ONLINE

For more activities on this topic, head to www. brightredbooks.net/N5German

LEARNING

SCHOOL SUBJECTS – DIE SCHULFÄCHER

In this section, we will look at the context of Learning. The topics we will cover include:

- school subjects and learning activities
- preparing for exams
- describing your school
- discussing school rules and uniform
- talking about the importance of language-learning.

ONLINE TEST ✔

Take the school subjects test at www.brightredbooks.net to see how many words for school subjects you can remember.

⚙ ACTIVITY: Lernmethoden – Learning techniques

Think about the activities you do in each subject. Can you work out what the following activities mean in English?

1   Ich lerne Vokabeln.
2   Ich löse Probleme.
3   Ich mache Gruppenarbeit.
4   Ich arbeite mit einem Partner/mit einer Partnerin.
5   Ich arbeite am Computer.
6   Ich schreibe Notizen.
7   Ich lese einen Text.
8   Ich schaue Wörter im Wörterbuch nach.
9   Ich recherchiere.
10 Ich schreibe Aufsätze.
11 Ich zeichne.

12 Ich gebe eine Präsentation.
13 Ich spiele ein Instrument.
14 Ich treibe Sport.
15 Ich verbessere mein Hörverständnis.
16 Ich übe Rechtschreibung.
17 Ich rechne im Kopf.
18 Ich bastele.
19 Ich koche.
20 Ich lerne Grammatik.
21 Ich bereite mich auf die Prüfungen vor.
22 Ich mache einen Versuch.

GIVING INFORMATION ABOUT YOUR SUBJECTS

You could say which subjects are compulsory:

> **EXAMPLE:**
>
> Die Pflichtfächer sind Mathe, Englisch, Religion, Sport und eine Fremdsprache.

You could talk about the subjects you are strong at and the ones you struggle with.

> **EXAMPLE:**
>
> Ich bekomme gute Noten in Geschichte. – I get good marks in History.
>
> Ich mache gute Fortschritte in Physik. – I am making good progress in Physics.
>
> Ich habe schlechte Noten in Mathe. – I get bad marks in Maths.
>
> Ich habe Schwierigkeiten in Erdkunde. – I have difficulties in Geography.

You could say how long you have been learning a subject using seit. This is a good grammar point to demonstrate, as the tenses used are different in the two languages:

> **EXAMPLE:**
>
> Ich lerne seit vier Jahren Deutsch. (present tense)
>
> I have been learning German for four years. (past tense)

ACTIVITY: Teachers

The teacher plays an important role in the learning process.

You come across an article where pupils in a class in Germany have done a survey on the qualities of a good teacher. Read the results and complete the task.

10:30 AM   75%

Class 8b were asked about the qualities of a good teacher. Here are the results:

EIN GUTER LEHRER ...	
hat einen Sinn für Humor	
kann alles gut erklären	20%
hat keine Lieblingsschüler in der Klasse	12%
unterrichtet gern	5%
ist geduldig, wenn wir etwas nicht verstehen	8%
macht den Unterricht relevant und realistisch	17%
gibt Strafarbeiten, nur wenn es nötig ist	10%
organisiert Ausflüge	4%
behandelt die Schüler wie normale Menschen und nicht wie Babys	9%
	15%

DON'T FORGET

In any writing assessment, you should try to use a range of verbs.

ONLINE

For more activities on this topic, head to www.brightredbooks.net/N5German

Explain the following percentages:

a 8%   **b** 20%   **c** 9%   **d** 12%   **e** 4%   **f** 5%

THINGS TO DO AND THINK ABOUT

1   Write a list of the subjects you are currently studying at school in German.
2   Beside each subject, write at least one activity that you do in this subject.
3   Write down whether you are getting good or bad marks, or whether you are making good progress or having difficulties.

PREPARING FOR EXAMS – DIE PRÜFUNGEN VORBEREITEN

In this section, you will look at how to prepare for exams.

SOME KEY VOCABULARY

- die Klassenarbeit – class test
- die Prüfung – exam
- bestehen – to pass
- durchfallen – to fail
- das Abitur – the school-leaving exam

TALKING ABOUT EXAMS

Let's start by thinking about how you might introduce talking about your exams:

- Dieses Jahr mache ich die Prüfungen National 5. – This year I am doing the National 5 exams.
- Ich muss viel lernen. – I have to study a lot.
- Es gibt so viel Druck im Moment. – There is so much pressure at the moment.
- Die Lehrer geben uns so viele Hausaufgaben. – The teachers give us so much homework.
- Die Prüfungen sind nur ein Gedächtnistest. – The exams are only a memory test.
- Man muss die Fakten auswendig lernen. – You have to learn the facts by heart.
- Ich lerne lieber allein. – I prefer studying by myself.
- Ich kann mich besser konzentrieren. – I can concentrate better.
- Ich lerne lieber mit Freunden zusammen. – I prefer studying with friends.
- Es ist gesellig. – It is sociable.
- Man kann ein Thema besprechen und einander testen. – You can discuss a topic and test each other.

⚙ ACTIVITY Study techniques

What study techniques do these teenagers use?

1 Ich mache einen Lernplan.
2 Ich lerne mit Freunden zusammen und wir testen einander.
3 Ich nehme Notizen mit meinem Handy auf.
4 Ich tippe Notizen auf meinem Computer ab.
5 Ich benutze verschiedene Lernmethoden.
6 Ich mache Übungen im Internet.
7 Ich lese meine Notizen durch, dann stellt mir meine Mutter ein paar Fragen.
8 Ich lerne die wichtigsten Ideen auswendig.
9 Ich surfe im Internet und recherchiere ein Thema.
10 Ich lese einen Text und dann schreibe ich Fragen auf.

ACTIVITY: Preparing for exams

You pick up a leaflet which gives advice about preparing for exams.

Read the German text and complete the questions below.

Wie kann man die Prüfungen überleben?

Das Abitur ist in einem Monat und die Schüler machen sich Sorgen. Sie leiden unter Stress und es gibt einfach zu viele Hausaufgaben. Sie wollen nicht durchfallen und sitzenbleiben.

Hier sind ein paar Ratschläge, wie man die Prüfungen überstehen kann:

1 Es ist wichtig, dass man Kontakt zu Freunden hat. Sie haben die gleichen Probleme und Sorgen.

Einige Tipps:

- Man kann miteinander reden.
- Man kann Ideen teilen.
- Man kann einander testen.
- Man kann einander Fragen stellen.
- Man kann einander eine SMS schreiben und einander Mut geben.

2 Die Entspannung ist sehr wichtig, besonders am Abend vor dem Examen. Man braucht Kraft. Am besten macht man einen Spaziergang an der frischen Luft. Oder man kann zu Hause Yoga üben, um die Nerven zu beruhigen. Man muss richtig atmen.

3 Es ist besser, wenn man die ganze Nacht durchschläft. Bevor man ins Bett geht, könnte man ein Bad nehmen oder schöne Musik hören. Man sagt auch, dass ein warmes Getränk mit viel Milch, z.B. Kakao beim Schlafen hilft.

4 Man muss gesund essen. Man sollte eine richtige Mahlzeit essen und keine Süßigkeiten naschen. Wenn möglich, soll das Essen viele Vitamine enthalten.

1 How do German pupils feel as the final exam approaches? Give two details.

2 How can your friends help you out? Give three details.

3 What other three pieces of advice are given? Explain the main message and give two details.

THINGS TO DO AND THINK ABOUT

Using the language you have learned in this section, write a short essay about how you prepare for exams: discuss what techniques you use but also how you prepare your mind and body.

DON'T FORGET

It is good to make use of modal verbs: *Ich kann* and *Ich muss.*

ONLINE

For more activities on this topic, head to www. brightredbooks.net/ N5German

ONLINE TEST

Try the online test at www.brightredbooks. net/N5German to further develop your knowledge of vocabulary about preparing for exams.

DESCRIBING MY SCHOOL – MEINE SCHULE BESCHREIBEN

In this section, we will look at some of the differences between Scottish and German schools. You will learn vocabulary through a reading and listening task to help you describe your own school.

DAS SCHULSYSTEM IN DEUTSCHLAND – THE GERMAN SCHOOL SYSTEM

German pupils go to primary school for four years:

die Grundschule = primary school

Then there is a choice of secondary school:

das Gymnasium = grammar school

die Realschule = secondary school

die Hauptschule = secondary school

die Gesamtschule = comprehensive school

In Germany, pupils talk about what class they are in to refer to how many years of education they have completed. In S4, you would say *Ich bin in der elften Klasse* because you are in your 11th year of education.

⚙ ACTIVITY Describing my school

Which school system is being described? Write *Schottland* or *Deutschland*:

1 Die Schule fängt um acht Uhr an.
2 Es gibt normalerweise keine Mittagspause.
3 Wir haben vier Jahre Grundschule.
4 Die Schule ist um Viertel nach drei aus.
5 Die Schüler haben ein Klassenzimmer.
6 Die Schüler tragen eine Uniform.
7 Die Schüler essen zu Mittag in der Kantine.
8 Wir haben schriftliche und mündliche Prüfungen in den meisten Fächern.
9 Die Schule ist oft um ein Uhr aus.
10 Die Schüler tragen keine Uniform.
11 Der Unterricht fängt um neun Uhr an.
12 Wir freuen uns auf den Wandertag.
13 Die Lehrer haben ihre eigenen Klassenzimmer.
14 Wir haben Herrn Schmidt für Mathe und Erdkunde.
15 Wenn der Mathelehrer krank ist, fällt der Unterricht aus.

 ACTIVITY: Karl's school

You receive an e-mail from your exchange partner Karl. He talks about his school. Read the German text and answer the questions that follow.

| 10:30 AM | 75% |

Mein Name ist Karl. Ich besuche ein Gymnasium in der Stadtmitte von Stuttgart. Ich gehe gern zur Schule. Ich habe viele Freunde in der Schule und es gibt viele AGs. Ich bin in der Volleyballmannschaft und ich bin Mitglied des Schulorchesters. Ich spiele Gitarre.

Die Pflichtfächer sind Mathe, Deutsch und eine Fremdsprache. Ich habe Kunst, Erdkunde, Physik und Biologie gewählt. Ich finde Biologie einfacher als Physik. Ich lerne nicht gern Physik, weil es so kompliziert ist. Der Lehrer gibt zu viele Hausaufgaben. Mein Lieblingsfach ist Kunst, weil es Spaß macht. Der Lehrer ist sehr sympathisch und unterrichtet gern.

Das Schulgebäude ist ziemlich alt. Die Klassenzimmer sind sehr klein und ganz dunkel. Es gibt eine schöne Bibliothek und eine neue Sporthalle. Die Aula ist furchtbar denn sie ist schmutzig und unordentlich.

Es gibt neunzig Lehrer. Die meisten Lehrer sind hilfsbereit und freundlich. Einige sind streng und ungeduldig. Es gibt tausend Schüler. Einige Schüler sind frech und faul aber die meisten sind fleißig und lustig.

Die Schule fängt um acht Uhr an und ist um Viertel nach eins aus. Es gibt zwei Pausen. Eine Pause dauert zehn Minuten und die andere dauert fünfzehn Minuten. In der Pause spreche ich mit meinen Freunden und ich esse ein Brötchen.

1. Why does Karl like going to school? Give two reasons.
2. Give four points he makes about school subjects.
3. Give four points he makes about the school building/facilities.
4. Give two points about the teachers.
5. Give two points about the pupils.
6. Give three points about the school day.

ACTIVITY: Listening: Tobias's school

Listen to the clip online to hear Tobias describing his school. Then answer the questions below.

The transcript can be found on p. 92.

1. What kind of school is it? (1)
2. Where is the school located? (2)
3. Why are Maths and German mentioned? (1)
4. Why is PE his favourite subject? (2)
5. Why does he not like History? (2)
6. What does he say about Chemistry? (1)
7. What is the school building like? (2)
8. Which facilities are described? (2)
9. Which club is he in, and how do we know he is successful? (2)

THINGS TO DO AND THINK ABOUT

Write a short essay describing your school. You could state whether you prefer the school system in Scotland or Germany. This would be a good opportunity to use the separable verb *vor/ziehen* = to prefer.

EXAMPLE

Ich **ziehe** das Schulsystem in Deutschland **vor**, weil die Schule um ein Uhr aus ist.

 DON'T FORGET

When doing a listening task, listen out for words that sound like English.

 ONLINE TEST

Try the online test to build up more vocabulary to describe your school.

 ONLINE

For more activities on this topic, head to www.brightredbooks.net/N5German

SCHOOL RULES – DIE SCHULREGELN

In this section, you will learn how to discuss the rules in your school and give your opinion on school uniform.

ACTIVITY Margit's opinions

Margit gives her opinions about the rules in her school. Translate the following rules.

Margit agrees with these rules:

1   Man darf Sportschuhe tragen.
2   Man muss den Computer ausschalten.
3   Man muss pünktlich zur Schule kommen.
4   Man muss auf den Treppen ordentlich gehen.
5   Man muss hilfsbereit und höflich sein.
6   Man darf nicht rauchen oder Drogen nehmen.
7   Messer sind streng verboten.
8   Mobbing ist streng verboten.

Margit does not agree with these rules

1   Man muss die Hausaufgaben machen.
2   Man darf im Unterricht nicht plaudern.
3   Man darf keinen Kaugummi kauen.
4   Man muss alle Schüler und Lehrer respektieren.
5   Man darf nicht schwänzen.
6   Man muss den Lehrern zuhören.

Can you understand these strange rules?

1   Man muss ein Haustier jeden Tag zur Schule mitbringen.
2   Man darf während des Unterrichts eine Bratwurst essen.
3   Man muss auf den Tisch schreiben.
4   Man darf Unsinn machen.
5   Man darf zu spät zum Unterricht kommen.
6   Man darf keine schwarze Kleidung tragen.
7   Man darf nie etwas Neues lernen.
8   Man darf kämpfen.

ACTIVITY Kaugummi

You read an interesting article about chewing gum in schools. Read the text and answer the questions.

Kaugummi in der Schule

Schüler wollen, dass das Kaugummikauen während der Prüfungen legalisiert werden sollte.

Kaugummikauen ist verboten, weil man so oft die Reste des Kaugummis unter den Tischen oder auf dem Boden findet.

Bei einer Befragung meinten erstaunlicherweise 60 Prozent der befragten Lehrer, dass sie nichts gegen Kaugummi hätten. Denn die positiven Eigenschaften eines Kaugummis sind, dass es gut gegen Übergewicht ist, Stress vermeidet und wach hält.

1   When do pupils want to be allowed to chew gum? (1)
2   Give one reason why chewing gum is banned in school. (1)
3   What was the surprising result of the survey about this? (1)
4   Name two advantages of chewing gum. (2)

⚙ ACTIVITY: School uniform

You read another article, this time about the advantages and disadvantages of school uniform. Read the text and answer the questions.

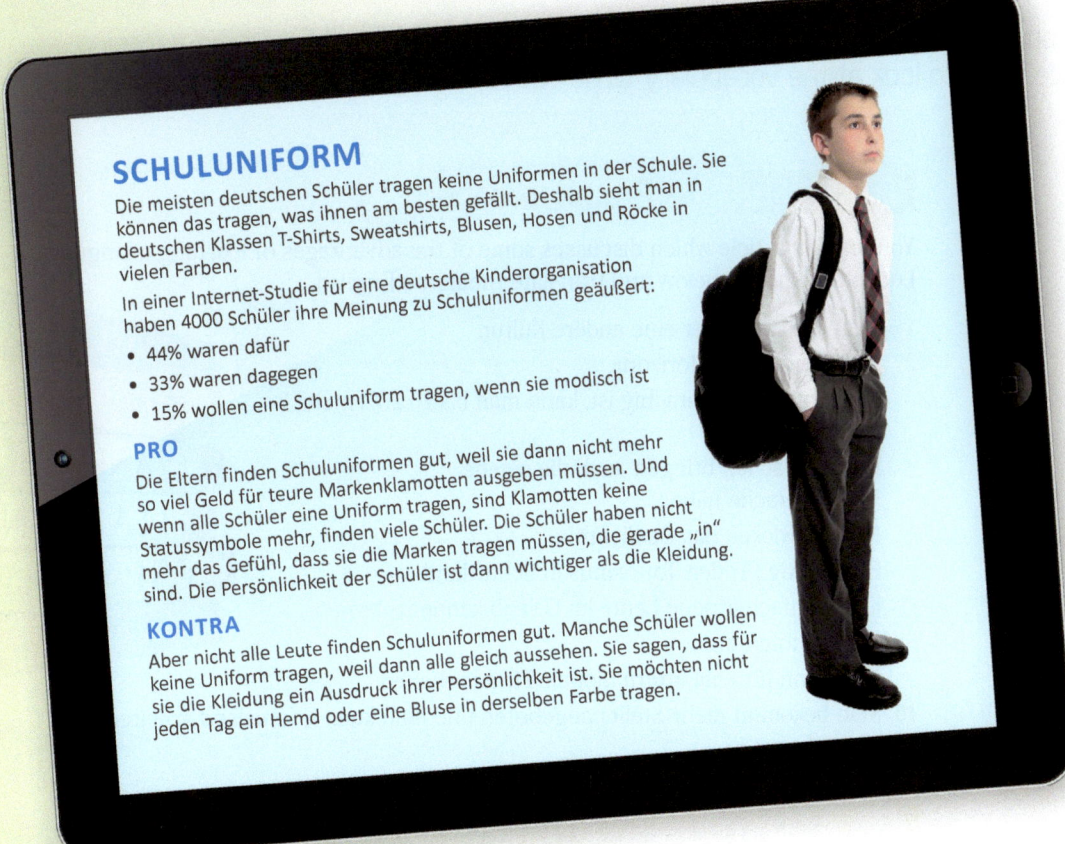

SCHULUNIFORM

Die meisten deutschen Schüler tragen keine Uniformen in der Schule. Sie können das tragen, was ihnen am besten gefällt. Deshalb sieht man in deutschen Klassen T-Shirts, Sweatshirts, Blusen, Hosen und Röcke in vielen Farben.

In einer Internet-Studie für eine deutsche Kinderorganisation haben 4000 Schüler ihre Meinung zu Schuluniformen geäußert:

- 44% waren dafür
- 33% waren dagegen
- 15% wollen eine Schuluniform tragen, wenn sie modisch ist

PRO

Die Eltern finden Schuluniformen gut, weil sie dann nicht mehr so viel Geld für teure Markenklamotten ausgeben müssen. Und wenn alle Schüler eine Uniform tragen, sind Klamotten keine Statussymbole mehr, finden viele Schüler. Die Schüler haben nicht mehr das Gefühl, dass sie die Marken tragen müssen, die gerade „in" sind. Die Persönlichkeit der Schüler ist dann wichtiger als die Kleidung.

KONTRA

Aber nicht alle Leute finden Schuluniformen gut. Manche Schüler wollen keine Uniform tragen, weil dann alle gleich aussehen. Sie sagen, dass für sie die Kleidung ein Ausdruck ihrer Persönlichkeit ist. Sie möchten nicht jeden Tag ein Hemd oder eine Bluse in derselben Farbe tragen.

1 What are the most common items of clothing worn by German pupils?

2 What was the opinion of 15% of those pupils surveyed?

3 Why are many parents happy with school uniform?

4 Why are many pupils in favour of uniform?

5 What argument is given against wearing uniform?

DON'T FORGET

Remember that the German word *man* can be translated in several ways: you, one or we.

THINGS TO DO AND THINK ABOUT

Write a short essay discussing the rules in your school. Remember that it is important to give your opinion about the rules: Ich finde die Regeln ... You should also try to use discursive language: Ich bin für die Uniform/Ich bin gegen die Uniform.

ONLINE TEST

Try the online test at www.brightredbooks.net/ N5German to get more practice at listening and reading texts before your assessment.

ONLINE

For more activities on this topic, head to www. brightredbooks.net/ N5German

LEARNING FOREIGN LANGUAGES – FREMDSPRACHEN LERNEN

In this section, you will learn how to discuss some of the advantages of learning a foreign language. We will also look at the vocabulary to do with spending a gap year abroad.

⚙ ACTIVITY Fremdsprachen

You read an article which discusses some of the advantages of learning a language. Look at the points below and translate them into English.

1   Man lernt viel über eine andere Kultur.
2   Es erweitert den Horizont.
3   Wenn man mehrsprachig ist, kann man bis zu 20% mehr Geld verdienen.
4   Fremdsprachen bringen auch die eigene Muttersprache näher.
5   Man entwickelt das Gedächtnis.
6   Es ist nötig für den Tourismus in Schottland.
7   Es ist einfacher neue Leute im Urlaub kennenzulernen.
8   Man ist toleranter.
9   Man kann für eine internationale Firma arbeiten.
10 Man bekommt mehr Stellenangeboten und man kann im Ausland arbeiten.

⚙ ACTIVITY The benefits of learning a foreign language

You read the following article about the benefits of learning a foreign language. Answer the questions in English:

Es lohnt sich, eine Fremdsprache zu lernen

Man lernt Sprachen, um mit Leuten in anderen Ländern sprechen zu können und ihre Kultur besser zu verstehen. Sprachen sind auch für das Arbeitsleben wichtig.

Schüler in Europa lernen im Durchschnitt 2.2 Fremdsprachen. In Großbritannien liegt der Durchschnitt niedriger als in allen anderen europäischen Ländern. Viele britische Schüler denken: "Fremdsprachen sind nicht so wichtig, weil alle Leute auf der Welt Englisch sprechen."

Falsch! 75% der Weltbevölkerung sprechen kein Englisch!

60% aller britischen Firmen haben Handelskontakte mit Ländern, in denen kein Englisch gesprochen wird. Das heißt: Wer eine Fremdsprache spricht, hat viel bessere Chancen, einen guten Beruf zu finden.

In welchen Gebieten hilft eine Fremdsprache? Hier sind einige Beispiele:

- Reisen und Tourismus
- Transportfirmen
- Technische Hilfsdienste für Kunden im Ausland
- Design von Webseiten und Prospekten
- Finanz und Verkauf

1   Which advantages of learning a foreign language are mentioned in the opening paragraph?
2   According to the article, what do many British teenagers think about language-learning?
3   Why is 75% mentioned?
4   Why might knowledge of a foreign language be useful in the workplace?
5   Mention four business sectors where knowledge of a foreign language would be useful.

SCHOOL EXCHANGES

One way of improving your language skills is to go on a school exchange.

 **ACTIVITY:** Exchange trip to Germany

In the following article, five Scottish teenagers give their opinions about an exchange trip to Germany. Summarise the texts in English.

Fünf Schüler aus Schottland sprechen über ihren Schüleraustausch in Deutschland

Julia

Man sagt oft, dass alle Leute Englisch sprechen, aber das stimmt nicht. Mein Partner und seine Familie sprachen wenig Englisch, und ich konnte ihr Deutsch nicht gut verstehen. Sie sprachen sehr schnell und ganz anders als mein Lehrer. Nach einer Woche habe ich sie besser verstanden. Man muss Geduld haben.

Chris

Der Schulaustausch war ein tolles Erlebnis. Ich habe mein Deutsch so oft wie möglich geübt. Ich wollte mein Deutsch verbessern. Zum Glück habe ich mich sehr gut mit meinem Partner verstanden. Wir hatten die gleichen Interessen und wir konnten viel darüber reden – über Sport, Musik und sogar Politik.

Rosie

Ich fand es nicht so gut, dass die schottischen Schüler oft zusammen waren. Wir haben Englisch gesprochen, und ich konnte nicht genug Deutsch üben. Ich möchte lieber allein nach Deutschland fahren und dort zur Schule gehen.

Carole

Mein Aufenthalt in Deutschland hat viel Spaß gemacht. Ich habe versucht, jeden Tag die Zeitung zu lesen. Ich habe neue Vokabeln notiert. Ich konnte meine Partnerin und ihre Eltern gut verstehen, da sie Hochdeutsch sprachen. Aber ich fand es schwer, die Oma zu verstehen. Sie hat oft Deutsch mit bayrischem Akzent gesprochen.

Richard

Seit dem Austausch arbeite ich viel mehr in den Deutschstunden. Ich habe gesehen, dass es Spaß macht, eine andere Sprache zu verstehen und zu sprechen. Die meisten deutschen Schüler lernen zwei Fremdsprachen und haben etwa acht Stunden Fremdsprachenunterricht pro Woche – das finde ich besser.

 DON'T FORGET

Remember to use *seit* and the present tense to say how long you have been learning a language: Ich lerne seit vier Jahren Deutsch.

 ONLINE TEST

Try the online test on language-learning at www.brightredbooks.net/N5German to develop your ideas even further.

 ONLINE

For more activities on this topic, head to www.brightredbooks.net/N5German

 ## THINGS TO DO AND THINK ABOUT

Try to answer the following questions in German:

1 Welche Fremdsprachen lernst du?

2 Seit wann lernst du diese Sprachen?

3 Welche Sprachen möchtest du lernen?

4 Findest du es wichtig, eine Fremdsprache zu lernen?

FUTURE PLANS – ZUKUNFTSPLÄNE

In this section, you will learn how to talk about your future plans as well as discuss the reasons why some students take a gap year.

⚙ ACTIVITY: Next year

What do these pupils intend to do next year?

1 Ich werde weiterstudieren.
2 Ich werde die Schule verlassen.
3 Ich werde eine Lehre machen.
4 Ich werde zur Uni gehen.
5 Ich werde mir einen Job suchen.
6 Ich werde eine Weltreise machen.
7 Ich werde zu einer technischen Hochschule gehen.
8 Ich werde ein Gap Jahr machen.

⚙ ACTIVITY: Future plans

Read what these German teenagers have to say about their future plans. Write three things about each person in English:

1 Hallo! Nächstes Jahr werde ich die Schule verlassen. Ich möchte in einem Supermarkt arbeiten und Geld verdienen. Dann werde ich mir eine Lehrstelle als Elektriker suchen.

2 Grüß dich! Ich werde meine Prüfungen machen. Wenn ich gute Noten bekomme, werde ich zur Uni gehen. Ich werde Medizin studieren.

3 Guten Tag! Ich werde eine Weltreise machen. Ich werde Australien und Indien besichtigen. Ich werde mir eine Stelle im Tourismus suchen.

FUTURE TENSE

German has a future tense which consists of the present tense of **werden** plus an infinitive (which is sent to the end of the sentence).

> **EXAMPLE:**
>
> Ich **werde** im Ausland **arbeiten**.   I will work abroad.
> Ich **werde** meine Fremdsprachen **benutzen**.   I will use my foreign languages.

GAP REISEN – TAKING A GAP YEAR

⚙ ACTIVITY: The benefits of a gap year

The following teenagers have all completed a gap year and discuss some of the benefits. Translate their statements into English.

Florian   Es erweitert den Horizont.
Gabi   Man wird selbstständiger.

Jonas	Man lernt ein neues Land und eine neue Kultur kennen.
Heike	Man kann Fremdsprachen lernen.
Hanna	Es ist ein Pluspunkt für den Lebenslauf.
Paul	Man wird toleranter und aufgeschlossener.
Max	Man entwickelt sein Selbstvertrauen.
Karl	Man lernt sein Geld einzuteilen.
Kerstin	Man kann neue Freunde und wichtige Kontakte machen.

DON'T FORGET

Remember to add 'er' onto the adjective to mean 'more': toleran**er** = more tolerant.

ACTIVITY: Gap year

You read an interesting article about the benefits and risks of doing a gap year. Answer the questions in English.

HAST DU VON GAP REISEN GEHÖRT?

Immer mehr junge Leute machen nach dem Gymnasium oder der Universität eine Gap Reise. Warum ist Gap Reisen so beliebt?

Wenn man nach der Schule nicht weiß, in welche Richtung sein Studium gehen soll, kann man sich ein Jahr Zeit lassen, um Entscheidungen zu treffen. Nach so viel Lernen wollen viele Schüler ein bisschen Freiheit und Auszeit. Mit der aktuellen schlechten Stellenaussicht denken manche Studenten, dass sie genauso gut eine Gap Reise machen.

Nach dem Abitur und dem Stress der Prüfungen kann man abschalten und sich entspannen. Nach einer Pause weiß man oft besser, was man als Beruf machen möchte. Unterwegs sieht man die Welt und man lernt Leute aus verschiedenen Ländern kennen. Außerdem sammelt man Erfahrung. Man lernt etwas über die Gewohnheiten und die Lebensweise einer anderen Kultur. Das ist bestimmt ein Pluspunkt für den Lebenslauf.

Das Problem ist, ob das Gap Reisen als Bereicherung oder Lücke im Lebenslauf bewertet wird. Manche Studenten haben Angst, dass Arbeitgeber diese Auszeit als Faulenzen betrachten werden. Einige Arbeitgeber finden Gap Reisen im Lebenslauf nicht so beeindruckend.

Aber das hängt meistens von der Qualität ab, was man in der Auszeit macht. Es ist wichtig, dass man etwas Sinnvolles während der Gap Reise macht, wie Freiwilligenarbeit. Oder man kann neue Fähigkeiten wie eine Fremdsprache erlernen.

Falko Loher aus Dortmund hat ein Jahr in einer Schule in China Englisch unterrichtet. Er wusste nicht ganz genau, was er an der Uni studieren wollte. Er interessierte sich für Geschichte und Politik und konnte sich nicht entscheiden, welches Fach er studieren wollte. Am Anfang war es schwierig für ihn eine andere Kultur kennen zu lernen und die neue Sprache zu beherrschen. Ein Lehrer in der Schule hat ihm zweimal in der Woche Privatunterricht gegeben. Jetzt kommt er mit der Sprache klar und er will Chinesisch an der Uni studieren. Nach einem Jahr in China ist Falko selbstständiger geworden und er hat jetzt mehr Selbstvertrauen. Er hofft, dass seine Erfahrung in China ihm später helfen wird, eine gute Stelle zu finden.

1. Give at least four reasons why students choose to do a gap year.
2. What is the main problem?
3. How can this problem be resolved?
4. Why did Falko Loher decide to do a gap year?
5. How has Falko benefited from his year in China?

 ONLINE TEST

Try out the online test to get more practice in the future tense at www.brightredbooks.net/N5German

 THINGS TO DO AND THINK ABOUT

Write a paragraph using the future tense about your future plans. You could mention whether you will be taking a gap year and the reasons for this.

 ONLINE

For more activities on this topic, head to www.brightredbooks.net/N5German

JOBS – BERUFE

In this section, you will revise the vocabulary to do with jobs and places of work.

⚙ ACTIVITY: Match up 1

Can you remember these jobs? Match up the German word with the English meaning.

1 Zahnärztin	A electrician
2 Lehrerin	B postman
3 Elektriker	C vet
4 Frisör, female Frisörin	D doctor
5 Ingenieur	E housewife
6 Briefträger	F dentist
7 Sekretärin	G waiter
8 Tierärztin	H engineer
9 Krankenschwester	I teacher
10 Verkäufer	J hairdresser
11 Mechaniker	K sales assistant
12 Arzt	L secretary
13 Kellner	M nurse
14 Hausfrau	N mechanic

DON'T FORGET

To form the female version of the job, you add '-in': Polizist**in**/Soldat**in**

ONLINE TEST

Take the online test at www.brightredbooks.net/N5German to revise some more jobs.

⚙ ACTIVITY: Which job?

Which job is asked about, and what comment is made?

1	Arzt?	Es ist gut bezahlt.	6	Briefträger?	Es ist spannend.
2	Lehrer?	Es ist stressig.	7	Feuerwehrmann?	Es ist gefährlich.
3	Friseur?	Es ist einfach.	8	Tierärztin	Es ist abwechslungsreich.
4	Zahnarzt?	Es ist anstrengend.	9	Ingenieur?	Es ist schwierig.
5	Verkäuferin?	Es ist todlangweilig.	10	Sekretärin?	Es ist schlecht bezahlt.

ACTIVITY: Sentence-building

Build a German sentence to explain why someone wants to do each job. Take the first part of the sentence from section A and complete the sentence with a phrase from section B. Look at the example:

EXAMPLE

Ich möchte Tierarzt werden, weil ich gern mit Tieren arbeite.

Section A

Ich möchte Tierarzt werden
Ich möchte Briefträger werden
Ich möchte Mechaniker werden
Ich möchte Lehrer werden
Ich möchte Arzt werden
Ich möchte Zahnarzt werden
, weil

Section B

ich gern im Freien bin.
man Kontakt zu Menschen hat.
der Job gut bezahlt ist.
ich gern mit Tieren arbeite.
ich etwas Praktisches machen will.
ich mit Kindern arbeiten will.

ACTIVITY: Match up 2

Match the place of work with the job.

1 in einem Büro	A Tierarzt
2 in einem Krankenhaus	B Briefträger
3 in einer Tierarztpraxis	C Sekretärin
4 in einem Geschäft	D Lehrer
5 in einer Polizeiwache	E Verkäuferin
6 in einer Gesamtschule	F Krankenschwester
7 im Freien	G Mechaniker
8 in einer Werkstatt	H Polizist

ACTIVITY: Where do these people work?

1 Ich arbeite in einer Gesamtschule.
2 Ich arbeite in einer Werkstatt.
3 Ich arbeite in einer Fabrik.
4 Ich arbeite in einem Krankenhaus.
5 Ich arbeite in einem Geschäft.
6 Ich arbeite in einer Zahnarztpraxis.

ONLINE

For more activities on this topic, head to www.brightredbooks.net/N5German

THINGS TO DO AND THINK ABOUT

Write down what jobs members of your family have.

EXAMPLE

Mein Vater ist Lehrer.
Meine Mutter ist Ärztin.

DON'T FORGET

The word for 'a' is not used in German when referring to jobs: *Ich bin Lehrer* – I am **a** teacher.

CAREERS ADVICE – BERUFSBERATUNG

In this section, you will learn to talk about the qualities and skills you need for certain jobs.

⚙ ACTIVITY Ideal jobs

What line of work are these people interested in?

1 Ich möchte mit Tieren arbeiten.
2 Ich möchte mit Kindern arbeiten.
3 Ich möchte in einem Büro arbeiten.
4 Ich möchte bei einer internationalen Firma arbeiten.
5 Ich möchte viel reisen und meine Fremdsprachen benutzen.
6 Ich möchte Kontakt zu Menschen haben.
7 Ich möchte viel Geld verdienen.
8 Ich möchte selbstständig sein.
9 Ich möchte im Freien arbeiten.
10 Ich möchte etwas Praktisches machen.

⚙ ACTIVITY Qualities

a What qualities do these people have?

1 Ich bin gesellig.
2 Ich bin vertrauenswürdig.
3 Ich bin verständnisvoll.
4 Ich bin immer pünktlich.
5 Ich bin wirklich geduldig.
6 Ich bin fleißig.
7 Ich bin hilfsbereit.
8 Ich bin motiviert und organisiert.
9 Ich bin kreativ.
10 Ich bin aktiv und lebendig.
11 Ich bin ehrlich.
12 Ich bin unternehmungslustig.

b Which qualities would you need for the following jobs? Choose from the German adjectives used above.

1 Lehrer
2 Krankenschwester
3 Ingenieur
4 Polizist
5 Elektriker

⚙ ACTIVITY Skills

What skills do these people have?

1 Ich habe gute Noten in den Wissenschaften.
2 Ich bin höflich und kann deutlich sprechen.
3 Ich habe gute Computerkenntnisse.
4 Ich spreche fließend Englisch und Deutsch.
5 Ich habe viel Geduld, besonders mit Kindern.
6 Ich arbeite gern in einem Team. Ich habe Teamgeist.
7 Ich kann gut zuhören.
8 Ich kann auf einen Termin hinarbeiten.

ACTIVITY: Careers leaflet

You find a careers leaflet which talks about the qualities needed for certain jobs. Read the leaflet and then answer the questions.

Was ist wichtiger in der Arbeitswelt? Gute Noten oder positive Charaktereigenschaften?

Wir haben den Experten gefragt.

Viele Charaktereigenschaften sind wichtig für die meisten Stellen. Menschen, die höflich und hilfsbereit sind, haben mehr Erfolg im allgemeinen als Menschen, die launisch, ungeduldig oder schlecht gelaunt sind. Alle mögen Kollegen, die freundlich und locker sind. Ein Sinn für Humor ist auch wichtig. Aber manche Berufe brauchen bestimmte Eigenschaften oder Fähigkeiten. Eine Empfangsdame muss deutlich sprechen können – aber eine gute Empfangsdame muss auch organisiert und angenehm sein. Ein guter Klempner kann Toiletten und Duschen reparieren – aber er sollte auch fleißig und ehrlich sein. Laut der Experten sind gute Noten aus der Schulzeit und positive Eigenschaften beide wichtig.

1 What question is asked at the start of the article?
2 What types of people are more successful?
3 What kind of colleagues do we like to work with?
4 Which two jobs are mentioned, and what qualities are linked to these jobs?

ACTIVITY: Apprenticeships

You next read an article about apprenticeships. Answer the questions.

Lehrling werden ist wieder cool

In drei Monaten wird Stefan die Schule verlassen. Er hat keine Lust, Student zu werden. „Man muss zu lange warten, bevor man Geld verdienen kann", sagt er. „Mein Bruder war vier Jahre lang Student und am Ende hatte er Schulden. Meine Eltern mussten ihm helfen."

Stefan hat sich für eine zwei-jährige Lehre als Mechaniker entschieden. Sein Ausbildungsplatz befindet sich in einer Werkstatt in seinem Dorf. Der Job gefällt ihm, weil er praktisch und abwechslungsreich ist. Um ein guter Mechaniker zu werden, muss man selbstständig und zuverlässig sein. Wichtig ist auch, dass man sich mit seinen Mitarbeitern gut versteht.

An drei Tagen in der Woche wird Stefan in die Berufsschule gehen müssen. Über die Schule ist er geteilter Meinung: Einerseits freut er sich auf den Kontakt mit anderen Lehrlingen, aber andererseits findet er die Praxis interessanter als die Theorie. In der Zukunft möchte er seine eigene Werkstatt besitzen. „Ich weiß, dass dieses Ziel sehr hoch ist, aber es ist erreichbar", sagt er.

1 Why does Stefan not want to become a student? Give two reasons.
2 Why does he like the job as mechanic?
3 Which qualities are necessary for the job of mechanic? Mention two things.
4 Stefan will have to attend college. He has mixed feelings about this. Why is this? Mention two things.
5 What is Stefan's ambition?
6 What does Stefan say about this ambition?

ONLINE

Go to www.brightredbooks.net/N5German to complete a careers form.

THINGS TO DO AND THINK ABOUT

Write a paragraph about your qualities and skills. You could also mention the types of work you are interested in. Make sure you get ideas from the exercises. This work will help prepare you for the job-application e-mail in the course assessment.

ONLINE TEST

Test yourself on this topic at www.brightredbooks.net/N5German

PART-TIME JOBS – TEILZEITJOBS 1

You might already have a part-time job, or you might be considering getting one to earn some money.

In German, a part-time job can be translated in two ways: *Ich habe einen Nebenjob* or *Ich habe einen Teilzeitjob*.

 **ACTIVITY** What job?

Read the following sentences and find out where each person works and what job they do.

1 Ich arbeite als Kellner in einem Restaurant.
2 Ich arbeite als Zimmermädchen in einem Hotel.
3 Ich arbeite als Verkäuferin in einem Kaufhaus.
4 Ich arbeite an der Kasse in einer Tankstelle.
5 Ich bin Babysitter und ich passe auf die Kinder meiner Nachbarn auf.
6 Ich trage Zeitungen aus. Ich arbeite draußen im Freien.

 **ACTIVITY** Job adverts – Anzeigen

Skim-read the following job adverts and try to pick out some key points: what the job is, the hours, the pay and anything else you can understand. Then answer these questions:

1 Which job would you apply for, and why?
2 Which job would you not apply for, and why?

Advert A

Mögen Sie feines Essen? Sind Sie fleißig und motiviert? Wir bieten eine Stelle als Kellner/Kellnerin in unserem Familienrestaurant an. Sie müssen über 16 Jahre alt sein. Sie werden zehn Stunden pro Woche arbeiten. Sie können kostenlos im Restaurant essen. Sie werden sieben Euro pro Stunde verdienen plus Trinkgeld dazu. Sie müssen bereit sein, abends zu arbeiten. Rufen Sie uns an: Tel: 0235 2453886

Advert B

Wir bieten eine Lehre in unserem Friseursalon an. Sie werden die Gelegenheit haben, die nötigen Fähigkeiten zu entwickeln. Sie müssen höflich, hilfsbereit und unternehmungslustig sein. Sie werden Termine vereinbaren, die Haare der Kunden waschen und an der Kasse arbeiten. Sie müssen am Samstag von neun Uhr morgens bis fünf Uhr abends arbeiten. Sie werden sechs Euro fünfzig pro Stunde verdienen. Tel: 0333 4389576

Advert C

Arbeiten Sie gern im Freien? Wir suchen junge Leute, die gern in unseren Parks arbeiten wollen. Sie müssen im Alter von 13 bis 16 Jahren sein. Sie müssen aktiv, ehrlich und pünktlich sein. Sie müssen die Pflanzen und die Blumen gießen. Sie werden eine Stunde nach der Schule arbeiten. Sie müssen die Erlaubnis Ihrer Eltern haben. Sie können in einem Park in der Nähe von Ihrem Haus arbeiten. Sie werden fünfunddreißig Euro pro Woche verdienen. Wenn Sie sich mehr darüber informieren wollen, rufen Sie uns einfach an. Tel: 0223 3990900

ACTIVITY: What do you do at work? – Was machst du auf der Arbeit?

If you already have a part-time job, or for the sake of the Writing exam you are pretending to have a part-time job, you might want to say what your responsibilities and duties are at work.

Read the following phrases and decide which job is being described. Some phrases can be used for more than one job. The jobs being described are:

Empfangschef/Empfangsdame; Kassierer/Kassiererin; Verkäufer/
Verkäuferin; Babysitter/Babysitterin; Kellner/Kellnerin

1   Ich muss die Regale auffüllen.
2   Ich muss die Kunden bedienen.
3   Ich muss mit dem Publikum arbeiten.
4   Ich muss mit Geld umgehen.
5   Ich muss Getränke, Zeitschriften und Chips verkaufen.
6   Ich muss Papiere sortieren.
7   Ich muss auf die Kinder aufpassen und die Hausarbeit machen.
8   Ich muss das Telefon beantworten.
9   Ich muss Butterbrote, Tee und Kaffee vorbereiten.
10 Ich muss Ausflüge reservieren.
11 Ich muss am Computer arbeiten.
12 Ich muss den Kindern mit ihren Hausaufgaben helfen.

ACTIVITY: When do you work? – Wann arbeitest du?

Listen to the people on the audio track talking about when they work, and note down:

1   the days they work
2   the hours they do
3   how much they earn per hour
4   how they get to work.

If you get stuck, read the transcripts below.

A: Ich arbeite am Montagnachmittag und Mittwochabend. Ich arbeite acht Stunden pro Woche und ich verdiene fünf Euro sechzig pro Stunde. Ich fahre mit der Bahn zur Arbeit.

B: Ich arbeite am Samstag von neun Uhr morgens bis fünf Uhr abends und am Sonntag von Mittag bis vier Uhr nachmittags. Ich arbeite zwölf Stunden pro Woche und ich verdiene sechs Euro zwanzig pro Stunde. Ich fahre mit dem Auto zur Arbeit.

C: Ich arbeite am Donnerstag nach der Schule und am Freitagabend. Ich arbeite sechs Stunden pro Woche und ich verdiene sieben Euro zehn pro Stunde. Ich fahre mit dem Rad zur Arbeit.

D: Ich arbeite zweimal in der Woche am Samstagmorgen und am Dienstagnachmittag. Ich arbeite fünf Stunden pro Woche und ich verdiene sechs Euro vierzig pro Stunde. Ich gehe zu Fuß zur Arbeit.

ONLINE TEST

Test how much you have learned about part-time jobs at www.brightredbooks.net/N5German

DON'T FORGET

Even if you don't have a part-time job, it is better to pretend to have one so that you have more to write about!

ONLINE

Follow the link at www.brightredbooks.net/N5German to search for job adverts in German.

THINGS TO DO AND THINK ABOUT

This is a chance for you to revise basic vocabulary such as days of the week, time phrases and numbers.

PART-TIME JOBS – TEILZEITJOBS 2

In this section, you will learn to talk about the advantages and disadvantages of having a part-time job as well as the kind of language that is used in job adverts.

 **ACTIVITY** For or against?

Are these people for or against having a part-time job?

1 Man wird selbstständiger.
2 Man lernt Teamgeist.
3 Ich bin noch zu jung.
4 Man kann neue Leute kennen lernen.
5 Ich habe zu viele Hausaufgaben.
6 Man lernt etwas über die Arbeitswelt.
7 Ich muss für die Prüfungen lernen.
8 Man lernt pünktlich zu sein.
9 Ich möchte mein eigenes Geld verdienen.
10 Man entwickelt sein Selbstvertrauen.
11 Ich habe keine Zeit für meine Freunde. Ich arbeite ständig.
12 Ich kann Geld für meinen Urlaub sparen.
13 Ich bin oft müde in der Schule.
14 Ich möchte Arbeitserfahrungen sammeln.
15 Ich möchte einen tollen Lebenslauf haben.

 **ACTIVITY**

Translate the following paragraphs into English. This is good training for Higher German. If there are sections you are unsure of, try to focus on picking out the main points from the texts. Use a dictionary to look up any unfamiliar words.

1 Ich arbeite als Kellnerin in einem Café in der Stadtmitte. Ich koche Tee und Kaffee und ich bediene die Kunden. Ich arbeite dreimal in der Woche und ich verdiene fünf Euro sechzig pro Stunde. Ich mag die Arbeit, weil sie einfach und abwechslungsreich ist. Es gibt immer viel zu tun. Mein Chef ist sehr geduldig und ich komme gut mit meinen Kollegen aus. Ich langweile mich nie und ich rede gern mit den Kunden.

2 Ich arbeite als Verkäuferin in einem Modegeschäft. Ich helfe den Kunden, ich fülle die Regale auf und ich arbeite an der Kasse. Was ich am besten mag, ist dass ich Ermäßigungen bekomme. Manchmal mag ich meine Arbeit nicht so gerne, weil meine Chefin oft gestresst und unhöflich ist. Ich muss viermal in der Woche arbeiten und deshalb habe ich nur wenig Freizeit. Mein Nebenjob ist auch schlecht bezahlt. Ich verdiene nur fünf Euro zwanzig pro Stunde.

3 Ich arbeite als Empfangsdame in einem Hotel an der Küste. Ich muss das Telefon beantworten und Ausflüge reservieren. Ich arbeite acht Stunden jeden Samstag. Die Arbeit ist gut bezahlt. Ich verdiene sieben Euro vierzig pro Stunde. Ich bekomme auch Trinkgeld dazu. Ich verstehe mich gut mit meinem Chef und meine Kollegen sind verständnisvoll und hilfsbereit.

ACTIVITY: Match up

It is important to be able to recognise the kind of language that appears in job adverts. This will be very useful for the Writing exam – the job application e-mail.

1 wir suchen	A written/in writing
2 ein gepflegtes Auftreten	B assistants
3 bewerben Sie sich	C good knowledge of computers
4 schriftlich	D we look forward to
5 der Lebenslauf	E interview
6 Aushilfskräfte	F we are looking for
7 wir freuen uns über	G we need
8 Mitarbeiter/Mitarbeiterinnen	H experience is necessary
9 wir brauchen	I CV
10 gute Computerkenntnisse	J a tidy appearance
11 Erfahrung erforderlich	K colleagues
12 das Vorstellungsgespräch	L apply to

ACTIVITY: Listening: Peter's part-time job

Listen to Peter talking about his part-time job, then answer the questions below.

1   Why does Peter need the money from a part-time job? (1)

2   a   What job does he do? (1)

    b   When does he work? (2)

3   a   Why does he mostly enjoy the job? (1)

    b   What negative aspects does he mention? (2)

4   What does he like best about the job? (1)

5   Why does he think that having a part-time job is a good idea? (3)

THINGS TO DO AND THINK ABOUT

Write a paragraph about your part-time job. Even if you don't have a part-time job, pretend that you do! Use language you have learned in this section to help you. Try to include the following:

- where you work
- what you do
- when you work
- how many hours you work
- how much you earn
- how you get to work
- your opinion of your part-time job
- any advantages or disadvantages there may be to having a part-time job and studying at the same time.

DON'T FORGET

Refer to the section on describing family members on pp. 6–9 – you can use the same vocabulary to describe your boss or colleagues.

ONLINE TEST

Test how much you have learned about part-time jobs at www.brightredbooks.net

VIDEO LINK

Check out the clips at www. brightredbooks.net/N5German for more on this topic.

WORK EXPERIENCE – ARBEITSPRAKTIKUM 1

In this section, you will learn to describe any work experience you have done. Although you may not have done any work experience yet, you need to be able to write about it in the Writing section of your exam, so use your imagination.

In German, there are two main ways of referring to your work experience: *Arbeitspraktikum* or *Betriebspraktikum*.

Let's start by thinking about where you might have done your work experience.

⚙ ACTIVITY Where did you work?

Read the following sentences, then work out where each person gained their work experience.

1 Ich habe mein Arbeitspraktikum in einem Büro gemacht.
2 Ich habe mein Arbeitspraktikum in einer Fabrik gemacht.
3 Ich habe mein Arbeitspraktikum in einem Geschäft gemacht.
4 Ich habe mein Arbeitspraktikum in einem Friseursalon gemacht.
5 Ich habe mein Arbeitspraktikum bei einer Autofirma gemacht.
6 Ich habe mein Arbeitspraktikum in einer Tierarztpraxis gemacht.

⚙ ACTIVITY Different work experiences

Read the following texts about different people's work experience. Then answer the following questions for each person:

1 Where did the person work?
2 What did the person think about their work experience?
3 What reason is given for this?

Silke

Ich habe zwei Wochen in einem Reisebüro gearbeitet. Es gelang mir, die Stelle zu finden, weil meine Nachbarin da arbeitet. Ich fand das Arbeitspraktikum sehr nützlich, weil ich viel gelernt habe – wie man Kunden anspricht, und warum gute Sprachkenntnisse sehr wichtig sind.

Lars

Mein Arbeitspraktikum war eine Zeitverschwendung. Ich war für zehn Tage bei einer Rechtsanwaltsfirma. Die Leute im Büro hatten zu viel zu tun und hatten keine Zeit für mich. Ich musste den ganzen Tag sitzen und zusehen. Ich habe nur Papiere fotokopiert und Kaffee gekocht. Nie wieder!

Christina

Mein Betriebspraktikum hat mir sehr geholfen, einige wichtige Entscheidungen zu treffen. Ich weiß jetzt, was ich später machen will und warum. Ich war für eine Woche in einem Kindergarten. Es hat so viel Spaß gemacht, mit Kindern zu arbeiten. Mein Lieblingsfach in der Schule ist Kunst. Ich habe Zeichnen und Basteln mit den Kindern gemacht. Ich habe auch gute Noten in Englisch und habe den Kindern englische Vokabeln beigebracht.

⚙ ACTIVITY: Stefan's work experience

Read the text and answer the questions in English.

Ich bin Stefan. Ich möchte Lehrer werden. Ich möchte mit Kindern arbeiten und lange Ferien haben. Ich bin hilfsbereit, freundlich und kreativ. Im Juni habe ich ein Arbeitspraktikum gemacht. Ich habe in einer Grundschule gearbeitet. Ich war zehn Tage dort. Ich habe das Arbeitspraktikum toll gefunden. Ich bin mit dem Bus dahin gefahren. Ich habe von acht Uhr bis ein Uhr gearbeitet. Meine Kollegen waren lustig und nett. Mein Chef war streng. Ich habe kein Geld verdient. Ich habe ein Geschenk bekommen.

1 What job does Stefan want to do? (1)
2 What are the reasons for this choice? (2)
3 What qualities does he have? (3)
4 When did he do his work experience? (1)
5 Where did he work? (1)
6 How long did he work there for? (1)
7 Did he enjoy the experience? (1)
8 What hours did he work? (2)
9 How were his fellow-workers? (2)
10 What was the boss like? (1)

⚙ ACTIVITY: Fill in the blanks

Copy out and fill in the missing words. Use the exercise above to help you.

Ich bin Heike. Ich _____ Sekretärin werden. Ich möchte am Computer _____ und in einem Büro arbeiten. Ich _____ fleißig und freundlich.

arbeiten   möchte   bin

Im Juni habe ich ein _____ gemacht. Ich _____ in einem Büro _____. Ich war zehn _____ dort. Ich habe das Arbeitspraktikum interessant _____. Ich bin mit dem Bus dahin _____. Ich habe von acht _____ bis drei Uhr gearbeitet. Meine Kollegen _____ lustig und nett. Mein Chef _____ gemein. Ich habe _____ Pfund verdient.

gefunden   Tage   waren   habe   Arbeitspraktikum

gearbeitet   war   gefahren   Uhr   fünfzig

⚙ ACTIVITY: What were you asked to do?

What tasks were these teenagers asked to do while on work experience?

1 Ich habe Kaffee gekocht.
2 Ich habe Papiere fotokopiert.
3 Ich habe das Telefon beantwortet.
4 Ich habe E-mails geschrieben.
5 Ich habe aufgeräumt.
6 Ich habe an der Kasse gearbeitet.
7 Ich habe die Kunden bedient.
8 Ich habe am Computer gearbeitet.
9 Ich habe mit den Kindern gespielt.
10 Ich habe Spiele und Ausflüge organisiert.

❗ THINGS TO DO AND THINK ABOUT

Write a paragraph in German about your own work experience. You should be able to adapt some of the sentences from the exercises above.

➕ **DON'T FORGET**

Remember to use a range of verbs in any talking or writing assessment.

 VIDEO LINK

Learn more about this topic by watching the clips at www.brightredbooks.net/ N5German

WORK EXPERIENCE – ARBEITSPRAKTIKUM 2

In this section, you will learn how to use both past tenses to talk about your work experience.

There are two main tenses that you will need to use when talking about the past. The perfect tense is used to talk about a completed action in the past. The other past tense is known as the simple past or imperfect tense. It is used to describe a repeated action in the past and is the tense used for descriptions.

THE PERFECT TENSE

The perfect tense is made up of two parts: (1) the auxiliary verb = the present tense of *haben* = to have or *sein* = to be; (2) a special verb form called the **past participle**.

The past participle is formed as follows. Start with an infinitive.

HABEN = TO HAVE	SEIN = TO BE
ich habe	ich bin
du hast	du bist
er/sie/es hat	er/sie/es ist
wir haben	wir sind
ihr habt	ihr seid
Sie haben	Sie sind
sie haben	sie sind

EXAMPLE:

spielen

You add the prefix **'ge-'** to the beginning of the infinitive, then remove the **'en'** and add **'t'** to the stem of the verb: ge <u>spiel</u> t = gespielt.

You need to know the present tense of *haben* and *sein*.

Most verbs take haben as the auxiliary verb:

Ich **habe** Tennis **gespielt**.

This can translate into English as I played, I have played, I did play.

Wir **haben** Federball **gespielt**.

Some verbs have a slightly irregular past participle. When the stem of the verb ends in **'t'** or **'d'**, the past participle ends in **'et'**.

EXAMPLE:

arbeiten = to work = gearbeitet

enden = to end = geendet

reden = to talk = geredet

Ich habe in einem Büro **gearbeitet**.

Die Arbeit hat um vier Uhr **geendet**.

Ich habe viel mit meinen Kollegen **geredet**.

Some verbs have an inseparable prefix. They make their past participles without adding **'ge-'**:

- besuchen/besichtigen – to visit
- beantworten – to answer
- verkaufen – to sell
- entwickeln – to develop

EXAMPLE

Ich habe die Sehenswürdigkeiten besichtigt. – I visited the tourist attractions.

Ich habe das Telefon beantwortet. – I answered the phone.

Ich habe mein Selbstvertrauen entwickelt. – I developed my self-confidence.

Verbs that end in **'-ieren'**, such as *organisieren, reservieren, reparieren, telefonieren*, do not add the prefix **'ge-'**.

EXAMPLE

Ich habe Ausflüge organisiert. – I organised excursions.

Ich habe Autos repariert. – I repaired cars.

ONLINE

Head to www. brightredbooks.net for more activities on this topic.

contd

Some verbs change in other ways and are known as strong verbs. For example, the vowel in the verb often changes. The past participle will start with '**ge-**' but will end in '**-en**'.

EXAMPLE

schreiben = to write = geschr**ie**ben   Ich habe E-mails geschrieben.

Here are some more useful verbs:

- verbringen = to spend (time) = verbracht
- beginnen = to start = begonnen
- bekommen = to get = bekommen

Some verbs take *sein* as the auxiliary verb. These verbs tend to denote motion from place to place.

EXAMPLE

gehen = to go = gegangen
Ich bin zu Fuß zur Arbeit gegangen.

fahren = to travel = gefahren
Ich bin mit dem Zug gefahren.

Other important verbs that take *sein* are:
bleiben = to stay = geblieben   werden = to become = geworden

EXAMPLE

Ich bin selbstständiger geworden.   I became more independent.

Now let's put the knowledge you have gained into practice.

essen	to eat	gegessen
finden	to find	gefunden
geben	to give	gegeben
helfen	to help	geholfen
lesen	to read	gelesen
nehmen	to take	genommen
schlafen	to sleep	geschlafen
sehen	to see	gesehen
singen	to sing	gesungen
sprechen	to speak	gesprochen
tragen	to wear/ carry	getragen
treffen	to meet	getroffen
trinken	to drink	getrunken
waschen	to wash	gewaschen

Here is a list of the most common past participles you need to learn.

ACTIVITY: Complete the passage

Complete the paragraph about work experience by filling in the correct past participle of the verb in brackets.

Ich habe mein Arbeitspraktikum im Mai _____ (machen). Ich habe in einem Büro _____ (arbeiten). Ich habe eine Woche dort _____ (verbringen). Ich bin zu Fuß zur Arbeit _____ (gehen). Die Arbeit hat um acht Uhr _____ (beginnen) und um vier Uhr _____ (enden). Ich habe viel _____ (lernen). Ich habe E-mails _____ (schreiben). Ich habe Kaffee _____ (kochen). Ich habe das Telefon _____ (beantworten). Das Arbeitspraktikum hat viel Spaß _____ (machen). Ich habe acht Euro pro Stunde _____ (verdienen). Ich habe mein Selbstvertrauen _____ (entwickeln) und ich bin selbstständiger _____ (werden).

THE IMPERFECT TENSE

The imperfect tense is used mainly for descriptions in the past. The most common verb you will use is *sein* = to be.

EXAMPLE

Die Arbeit **war** interessant. The work was interesting.

Der Chef **war** hilfsbereit.   The boss was helpful.

Meine Kollegen **waren** verständnisvoll.   My colleagues were understanding.

Note that *es gibt* = 'there is' becomes *es gab* = 'there was'.
Es **gab** viel zu tun.   There was lots to do.

THINGS TO DO AND THINK ABOUT

Write sentences for each of the following in the perfect tense:

- five *haben* verbs with regular past participles
- five *haben* verbs with irregular past participles
- three verbs that take *sein*.

DON'T FORGET

Remember to use a range of verbs: regular and irregular, verbs that take *haben* and others that take *sein*.

VIDEO LINK

Watch the clip at www.brightredbooks.net/N5German for more on this topic.

ONLINE TEST

Test yourself on the past tense at www.brightredbooks.net/N5German

CULTURE

HOLIDAYS – DIE FERIEN 1

In this section, you will learn to give your opinions on travelling as well as talk about holidays.

ACTIVITY Why do these people choose to travel?

1. Ich reise gern, um Abwechslung zu haben.
2. Ich reise gern, um dem schlechten Wetter zu entfliehen.
3. Ich reise gern, um viel Spaß zu haben.
4. Ich reise gern, um abzuschalten.
5. Ich reise gern, um meine Fremdsprachen zu verbessern.
6. Ich reise gern, um eine andere Kultur kennen zu lernen.
7. Ich reise gern, um andere Länder zu erleben.
8. Ich reise gern, um aus dem Alltag herauszukommen.
9. Ich reise gern, um ein Abenteuer zu haben.
10. Ich reise gern, um mich zu entspannen.

ACTIVITY When do these people go on holiday?

1. Ich fahre jedes Jahr in den Urlaub.
2. Ich fahre in den Sommerferien in den Urlaub.
3. Ich fahre im Hochsaison in den Urlaub.
4. Ich fahre im Herbst in den Urlaub.
5. Ich fahre in den Osterferien in den Urlaub.
6. Ich fahre im Frühling in den Urlaub.
7. Ich fahre in den Weihnachtsferien in den Urlaub.
8. Ich fahre Anfang Juli in den Urlaub.

ACTIVITY Why do people choose certain destinations?

1. Die Strände sind ausgezeichnet.
2. Die Sonne scheint jeden Tag.
3. Das Nachtleben ist wunderbar.
4. Es gibt eine gute Auswahl von Geschäften.
5. Es gibt viel zu tun und sehen.
6. Es gibt viele Sehenswürdigkeiten.
7. Es gibt einen riesengroßen Wasserpark.
8. Ich interessiere mich für die Kultur und die Sprache.
9. Die Leute sind sehr gastfreundlich.
10. Das Essen ist köstlich.

TALKING AND WRITING ABOUT HOLIDAYS: GRAMMAR RULES

Where: translating the word 'to'

Most countries are neuter, and the word for 'to' is *nach*:

> **EXAMPLE**
>
> Ich fahre **nach** Deutschland/Spanien/Italien/Griechenland.

Some countries are feminine, and the word for 'to' is *in die*:

> **EXAMPLE**
>
> Ich fahre **in die** Türkei/Schweiz.

Some countries are plural words, and the word for 'to' is *in die*:

> **EXAMPLE**
>
> Ich fahre **in die** Vereinigten Staaten/Niederlande.

You also use *nach* with towns:

> **EXAMPLE**
>
> Ich fahre **nach** New York.

TMP

You also need to remember the 1 Time, 2 Manner, 3 Place (TMP) rule.

Manner can refer to how you travel as well as who you travel with:

Ich fahre 1 im Juli 2 mit meiner Familie 3 nach Griechenland.

Ich fahre 1 im März 2 mit der Fähre 3 nach Dänemark.

ACTIVITY: Heike's holidays

Heike talks about her annual family holiday as well as her dream holiday.

Listen to the text and answer the questions in English.

1 When does Heike go on holiday? (1)

2 What accommodation does the family choose? (3)

3 What do they do

   a during the day? (1)   b at night? (2)

4 Give one advantage and three disadvantages of going on holiday with parents. (4)

5 Why does Heike want to go on holiday with her best friend Gabi? Give three reasons. (3)

6 What would they do on holiday? (2)

THINGS TO DO AND THINK ABOUT

Write about your summer holiday. You could mention:

- when and where you are going
- why you like to go there
- how you travel and why
- what accommodation you like to stay in and what the facilities are like
- what activities you do when on holiday.

DON'T FORGET

Remember to show off as many grammar points as you can in any writing or talking task you do.

ONLINE

For more activities on this topic, head to www.brightredbooks.net/N5German

ONLINE TEST

Try the online test at www.brightredbooks.net/N5German to revise the vocabulary for transport, accommodation and holiday activities.

HOLIDAYS – DIE FERIEN 2

 ACTIVITY: German holidays

You read an article about the type of holidays German people prefer. Read the text and answer the questions in English.

10:30 AM   75%

Die Deutschen sind bekanntlich ein reiselustiges Volk – in den Ferienwochen im Sommer tummeln sich in den Urlaubsregionen in Italien, Spanien und Kroatien jede Menge Gäste aus Deutschland.

Die Deutschen fahren am liebsten ans Meer. Einer Umfrage zufolge fahren 63% der Deutschen an die Strände von Nordsee, Ostsee und Mittelmeer. Nur 12% planen eine Reise in die Berge.

Wegen der Finanzkrise verbringen immer mehr Deutsche die Ferien in Deutschland. Die Lieblingsstädte in Deutschland sind München, Köln und Hamburg. Diese Städte haben nicht nur die besten Sehenswürdigkeiten, sondern auch die besten Unterhaltungsmöglichkeiten und Sportmöglichkeiten.

16% der Deutschen, die zu Hause bleiben, geben die höhern Energiekosten als Grund an. Mit einer erhöhten Sensibiltät für ökologische Folgen scheint das wenig zu tun zu haben. Nur 10% der Befragten sagten, sie hatten sich durch den Klimawandel bei der Reiseplanung beeinflussen lassen. Diese Planung geschieht immer häufiger per Internet. Nur 18% gaben an mit Hilfe eines Reisebüros ihren Urlaub organisiert zu haben.

Warum fahren die Deutschen in den Urlaub? Ein Hauptgrund ist der Tapetenwechsel. Man hat die Möglichkeit die gewohnte Umgebung hinter sich zu lassen. Man kann den Alltag, seine Sorgen und Probleme vergessen. Ein anderer Vorteil ist, dass man keine Hausarbeit machen muss, keine Betten machen, kein Abwaschen. Für viele Leute ist ein Urlaub gut für die Gesundheit. Man kann sich entspannen und sich erholen. Man kann die Sonne und die frische Luft genießen. Nur sollte man nicht zu lange in der Sonne liegen – Sonnenbrand kann ganz gefährlich sein.

Oft wählen Urlauber ihr Reiseziel wegen eines Hobbys – Bergwanderer, Segler, Reiter, Radfahrer, Angler oder

Taucher haben alle ihre Lieblingsorten, wo sie ihre Aktivitäten am besten unternehmen können. Andere Leute wollen neue Menschen kennen lernen und ihren Freundenkreis erweitern. Sie mögen netten Small Talk über Dies und Das.

Was ärgert die Deutschen am meisten im Urlaub? Auf dem ersten Platz sind die Warteschlangen vor dem Check-in-Schalter am Flughafen. Auf dem zweiten Platz sind die Staus auf der Autobahn. Man sollte seine Reise genau planen. Hier sind Navigationsgeräte sehr sinnvoll. Auf dem dritten Platz sind Mitmenschen, die sich wegen übermäßigem Alkoholkonsum schlecht benehmen.

1 Which countries do German people tend to visit? (3)
2 Explain the following percentages: (4)
   a 63%   **b** 12%   **c** 16%   **d** 18%
3 Why are the towns of Munich, Cologne and Hamburg so popular? (3)
4 Why do Germans go on holiday? Give four reasons. (4)
5 What influences holidaymakers in choosing their holiday? Discuss the two main types mentioned. (4)
6 What three things annoy Germans most on holiday? (3)

HOLIDAYS IN THE PRESENT TENSE

Saying where you normally go on holiday

Jedes Jahr fahre ich im Juli mit meiner Familie in die Türkei.

(Note the word order: when – who with – where)

Saying how you travel

Wir fahren mit dem Flugzeug dorthin.

contd

Saying where you stay

Wir wohnen in einem Hotel. Das Hotel hat ein tolles Freibad und drei Restaurants.

Saying what activities you do

Tagsüber gehe ich zum Strand und ich sonne mich. Ich bade im Meer.
Wir machen einen Spaziergang oder eine Radtour.

Abends gehe ich in die Stadt und ich esse im Restaurant.

Describing the holiday

Das Wetter ist warm und sonnig. Die Leute sind freundlich. Das Essen ist lecker.

TALKING ABOUT A PAST HOLIDAY

Saying where you went

Letztes Jahr bin ich mit meinen Eltern nach Griechenland gefahren.

Saying how you travelled

Wir sind mit dem Wagen und mit dem Schiff gefahren.

Saying where you stayed

Ich habe in einem Viersternehotel gewohnt.

Saying what activities you did

Jeden Tag bin ich zum Strand gegangen und ich habe mich gesonnt. Ich habe im Meer gebadet. Nachmittags habe ich einen Spaziergang/ eine Radtour gemacht.

Abends bin ich in die Stadt gegangen und ich habe in einem Restaurant gegessen.

Describing the holiday

Das Wetter war warm und sonnig. Es hat nicht geregnet. Die Leute waren sehr nett. Das Essen war lecker. Es war ein tolles Erlebnis. Es hat Spaß gemacht.

ACTIVITY: Jedes/Letztes Jahr

Write the headings 'jedes Jahr' = every year and 'letztes Jahr' = last year and then copy each sentence under the correct heading. You will need to pay attention to the tense the sentence is written in.

- Abends gehe ich zum Freizeitpark.
- Ich habe in einer Ferienwohnung gewohnt.
- Ich gehe zum Strand.
- Ich fahre mit meinen Eltern in die Türkei.
- Ich habe Volleyball am Strand gespielt.
- Die Leute sind freundlich.
- Ich fahre mit dem Auto.
- Ich bin mit meiner Familie nach Spanien gefahren.

- Es hat Spaß gemacht.
- Ich bade im Meer.
- Ich habe die Sehenswürdigkeiten besichtigt.
- Das Essen war lecker.
- Ich fahre mit dem Schiff.
- Ich wohne in einem Wohnwagen auf dem Campingplatz.
- Jeden Abend sind wir in die Disko gegangen.

DON'T FORGET

For extra practice, you could write the sentences out in a more structured way to form a story.

DON'T FORGET

In any writing or talking task, you should try where possible to include a range of tenses.

ONLINE

For more activities on this topic, head to www.brightredbooks.net/N5German

ONLINE TEST

Test yourself further on this topic at www.brightredbooks.net

THINGS TO DO AND THINK ABOUT

Write a paragraph to describe a holiday that you have enjoyed. Remember to make use of the perfect and imperfect tenses.

LITERATURE AND CINEMA – LITERATUR UND KINO

CINEMA

ACTIVITY War Horse

Read the text and complete the tasks that follow.

> Hast du den Film War Horse gesehen?
>
> Der Film erzählt die Geschichte von einem Pferd (Joey) im Ersten Weltkrieg. Joey ist das Pferd von Albert. Albert wohnt mit seiner Familie auf einem Bauernhof. Zu Beginn der Ersten Weltkriegs verkauft der Vater von Albert das Pferd an die Armee. Albert ist sehr traurig und er geht auch in den Krieg.
>
> Das Pferd und sein englischer Offizier werden in Frankreich an der Westfront stationiert. Der Offizier wird an der Front getötet. Das Pferd wird schwer verletzt aber von den Franzosen gepflegt. Als er wieder gesund ist, wird Joey von deutschen Soldaten konfiziert und geht wieder an die Front.
>
> Das Pferd interessiert sich nicht für den Krieg. Das Pferd will nur, dass sein Reiter gut zu ihm ist. Das Pferd sieht den Schrecken des Kriegs aber es erlebt auch die Wärme der Menschen. Die Frage: Wird Albert das Pferd am Ende des Kriegs wiedersehen?

ONLINE

For more activities on this topic, visit www.brightredbooks.net/N5German

Task A

Complete the English translation of the story of War Horse. Write down the numbers 1–10 then write the missing English word for each one.

> Have you seen the film War Horse?
>
> The film tells the 1 _____ of a horse (Joey) in the First World War. Joey is Albert's horse. Albert lives with his family on a 2 _____. At the beginning of the First World War, Albert's father 3 _____ the horse to the army.
>
> Albert is very 4 _____ and he also goes to war.
>
> The horse and his English officer are stationed in 5 _____ on the Western Front. The officer is killed on the front line. The horse is badly 6 _____ and is looked after by the French. When he is 7 _____, Joey is taken by the German officers and sent back to the front line.
>
> The horse is not interested in the 8 _____. The horse only wants his 9 _____ to be good to him. The horse sees the horror of war but also experiences the 10 _____ of humans. The question is: will Albert see the horse again at the end of the war?

Task B

What do these German teenagers have to say about the film?

Max	Der Film war gruselig.
Gabi	Ich fand den Film spannend.
Florian	Die Musik war klasse.
Thomas	Die Spezialeffekte waren toll.
Luisa	Ich fand den Film kindisch.
Jonas	Für mich war der Film zu sentimental.
Mia	Der Film war sehr traurig. Ich habe geweint.
Kevin	Die Geschichte war ein bißchen seltsam und unglaublich.

contd

Writing about a film

Here is some key vocabulary for writing about a film you have seen:

- Ich habe neulich den Film ... gesehen. – I have recently seen the film ...
- Der Film hat mir sehr gut gefallen. – I enjoyed the film.
- Der Film hat mir nicht gut gefallen. – I did not enjoy the film.
- Der Film geht um ... – The film is about ...
- die Liebe – love

- den Krieg – war
- ein Abenteuer – adventure
- Die Geschichte ist ... – The story is ...
- Die Schauspieler sind ... – The actors are ...
- Die Musik ist ... – The music is ...
- Die Spezialeffekte sind ... – The special effects are ...

DON'T FORGET

Remember to make use of your reading techniques. First look for cognates (words like English), then see if you can recognise any of the German words.

 ONLINE TEST

Take the online test about cinema at www.brightredbooks.net/N5German

LITERATUR

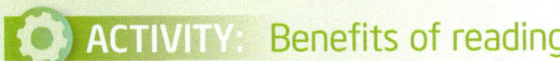 **ACTIVITY:** Benefits of reading

You read a leaflet explaining the benefits of reading.

6 Gründe, warum man Bücher lesen sollte!

1 Lesen kann gegen die Krankheit Alzheimer helfen. Durch regelmäßiges Lesen kann man im Alter länger mental fit bleiben. Durch Lesen wird das Gehirn gefordert und das Gedächtnis trainiert.

2 Durch Lesen kann man sich entspannen. Man kann dem Alltag entfliehen und in die Welt der Fantasie reisen.

3 Das Lesen bildet. Durch regelmäßiges Lesen erweitert sich der Wortschatz automatisch.

4 Viele Menschen haben Schwierigkeiten beim Einschlafen. Sie können nicht abschalten. Wenn man ein Buch zur Hand nimmt und einige Seiten liest, kommt man mental zur Ruhe.

5 Das Lesen hat einen positiven Einfluss auf die Kreativität. Durch das Abtauchen in die Welt der Fantasie entwickelt man die Vorstellungskraft.

6 Das Lesen erweitert den Horizont. Geschichten geben Einblick in das Leben anderer, in ihre Gedanken, ihre Arbeit und Gewohnheiten. Man lernt ferne Orte kennen und erlebt fremde Kulturen.

Summarise in English the main benefits of reading.

 ACTIVITY: Anne Frank

Anne Frank lived in Amsterdam during the Second World War. Mia, a 16-year-old girl, writes about the story of Anne Frank and the effect it had on her.

1 For which group of young people is the story of Anne Frank still an inspiration today? (2)

2 What facts prove that Anne Frank is popular? Give two facts. (2)

3 Why did Mia identify with Anne Frank? (1)

4 What did Mia like most about Anne Frank's diary? (1)

5 Why is Anne Frank a good role model for young people today? Give two reasons. (2)

Die Geschichte von Anne Frank, dem kleinen Mädchen, das in den Kriegsjahren ein Tagesbuch geführt hat, ist weltberühmt. Die Geschichte dient noch als Inspiration für alle Jugendlichen, die schwierige oder gefährliche Situationen überwinden müssen. Man hat das Buch schon in über 600 Sprachen übersetzt, und das Anne-Frank-Haus in Amsterdam lockt jedes Jahr über 800 000 Besucher aus der ganzen Welt an.

Ich habe mich sofort mit Anne Frank identifiziert. Anne hatte ein schwieriges Verhältnis zu ihrer älteren Schwester – genauso wie ich zu meiner Schwester. Anne schreibt offen über typische Jugendprobleme, und genau das hat mir so gut gefallen. Gerade für Jugendliche ist Anne Frank ein gutes Vorbild. Sie glaubt an das Gute in Menschen, sie spricht nie über Hass.

 THINGS TO DO AND THINK ABOUT

Write a short paragraph in German about a film that you have seen recently.

 VIDEO LINK

Check out the clip at www.brightredbooks.net/N5German for more on this topic.

FESTIVALS – FESTE

Festivals form an important part of any country's culture. Let's have a look at the vocabulary needed to talk about festivals.

KEY VOCABULARY

- die Karnevalszeit – carnival time
- Fasching – the word for carnival time in southern Germany
- närrisch – foolish
- der Narr – fool
- verkleidet – dressed up/disguised
- Die Leute ziehen durch die Straßen. – The people parade through the streets.
- der Umzug – parade
- teil/nehmen – to take part in
- feiern – to celebrate
- ein alter Brauch – an old tradition
- die Kostüme – costume
- die Maske – mask

 **ACTIVITY** Carnival

Read the following texts about festivals and answer the questions in English:

ES WIRD GEFEIERT

Fastnacht, Fasching, Karneval: Diese Kostümfeste haben viele Namen. Die Deutschen lieben die Karnevalszeit. Die Menschen verkleiden sich, tanzen auf den Straßen und veranstalten kilometerlange 'närrische' Umzüge.

Die Ursprünge der Karnevalszeit liegen im Frühlingsfest der alten Germanen. Die alten Germanen glaubten an Dämonen. Jeden Frühling feierten sie ein wildes Fest, bei dem die Wintergeister vertrieben werden sollten. Nach so viel Frieren, Frost und Schnupfen, hatten die Germanen einfach keine Lust mehr auf die kalte Jahreszeit. Das Fest war ein lautes und buntes Treiben. Die Dorfbewohner setzten sich grauenvolle Masken auf ihre Gesichter. Heutzutage tragen immer mehr Menschen eine Teufelsmaske. Man sieht auch oft Tiermasken. Die Tiere repräsentieren bestimmte Sünden, die ebenfalls vertrieben werden sollten. Der Esel bedeutet Trägheit und der Fuchs Geiz.

1 What do German people do at carnival time? (3)
2 What are the origins of carnival time? (2)
3 What types of masks have become popular? (2)

⚙ ACTIVITY: Oktoberfest

Read the German text and answer the English questions.

Das Oktoberfest in München

Heute gilt das Oktoberfest – das Fest der Landeshauptstadt München – als größtes Volksfest der Welt und ist weltweit bekannt. Das Oktoberfest ist etwas besonderes, weil es nicht nur ein Fest für die Münchner ist sondern auch eine internationale Großveranstaltung. Die typische Mischung aus Hightech und Tradition prägt heute das Fest und macht seine große Attraktivität aus.

Ursprünglich geplant als festlicher Anlass für eine bayrische Prinzenhochzeit, fand man schnell Gefallen an einem jährlich stattfindenden Volksfest, zu dem sich in wenigen Jahren Schausteller und Brauereien gesellten und so das Oktoberfest prägten, wie man es bis heute kennt.

Hier sind ein paar interessante Fakten.

- Besucher: **6,9 Millionen**
- Speziell für das Münchner Oktoberfest wird von den Münchner Brauereien ein eigenes Bier (Wiesn-Mätzn) mit höherem **Alkoholgehalt** gebraut.
- Jährlich arbeiten etwa **12.000 Personen** auf dem Oktoberfest davon 1.600 Kellner und Kellnerinnen.
- Es gibt insgesamt rund **104.000 Sitzplätze.**
- Es werden durchschnittlich **60.000 Hektoliter Bier** und **500.000 Brathähnchen** verkauft.
- Jährlich fallen auf dem Oktoberfest knapp **1.000 Tonnen Restmüll** an.

- Die rund 6,9 Millionen Besucher geben in den 16 Tagen insgesamt etwa **435 Millionen Euro** (pro Person durchschnittlich 63 Euro) auf dem Oktoberfest direkt aus.
- 2014 gab es **4.900 Fundsachen**, darunter 1.220 Kleidungsstücke, 1.155 Ausweise und Kreditkarten, 555 Geldbörsen, 420 Mobiltelefone, 280 Taschen, Rucksäcke und Beutel, 410 Schlüssel.

1 What makes the October festival so special? (2)
2 What makes the festival attractive? (1)
3 Why was the original festival planned? (1)
4 What are the two main groups represented? (2)

Now translate the facts from the bullet points above.

DON'T FORGET

Watch out for the words before a number that mean 'about': *rund/knapp/etwa.*

⚙ ACTIVITY: Der Jahresmarkt – Fairground

Part of any festival is a fairground. Can you work out what the following fairground attractions are? Match up the German and English words:

1 das Riesenrad	A dodgems
2 die Geisterbahn	B merry-go-round
3 die Schiffschaukel	C big wheel
4 die Achterbahn	D swing boat
5 der Autoscooter	E big dipper
6 das Karussell	F ghost train

ONLINE TEST

Take the online test to get more practice in festival vocabulary at www.brightredbooks.net/N5German

ONLINE

Check out the link at www.brightredbooks.net/N5German for more on Oktoberfest.

THINGS TO DO AND THINK ABOUT

Do some research on other festivals in Germany. The more background knowledge you have about Germany, the more it will help you with your listening and reading exams.

COURSE ASSESSMENT: WRITING

OVERVIEW OF COURSE ASSESSMENT

The Course assessment at National 5 will take the form of an Assignment (writing assessment), a Performance (talking assessment) and two question papers allowing you to demonstrate your reading, writing and listening skills in German.

COMPONENT 4: ASSIGNMENT – WRITING

You will be asked to produce a piece of writing of 120–200 words in the Modern Language using detailed language based on one of the following contexts: society, learning or culture. The context of employability will be assessed in Question paper 1. Throughout the year, you will prepare written pieces of work based on the topics studied which will help you to prepare for the assignment –writing.

The assignment – writing is:

- set by your centre within SQA guidelines
- conducted under a high degree of supervision and control in the classroom
- externally marked by SQA

The assignment – writing has a total mark allocation of 20 marks, which is scaled to 15 marks.

ONLINE

Head to the BrightRED Digital Zone and find a link to the SQA's marking instructions to give you an idea of how these parts will be assessed.

COMPONENT 5: PERFORMANCE – TALKING

You will be assessed on at least two of these four contexts: society, learning, employability, and culture.

The Performance will allow you to demonstrate your ability to communicate orally in German. After studying the topics at National 5, you will have prepared written pieces of work that should help you with your Performance. The Performance is made up of two parts:

- presentation – 10 marks
- conversation – 20 marks.

Presentation

You will be required to give a spoken presentation in German, using detailed language on a topic chosen from one of the following contexts:

- society
- learning
- employability
- culture.

You will choose the topic and develop it into a short presentation of approximately 1–2 minutes to allow demonstration of your language skills, accuracy, pronunciation and intonation.

You will be allowed to refer to up to five headings of no more than eight words each as prompts during the presentation and/or use visual aids. The headings may be in German or English.

You teacher/lecturer will listen to your presentation and ask questions based on it in order to engage you in a conversation on the topic.

Conversation

Following the prepared presentation and any follow-on questions, you will be required to take part in a conversation using detailed language on a different topic and context and to respond to some questions on that topic. The information to be exchanged will be mainly of a factual nature, but should also include some ideas and opinions. You should also ask questions where appropriate during the conversation.

Within this section, marks will be awarded as follows:

- conversation – 15 marks
- ability to sustain the conversation – 5 marks.

contd

Now you should know:

- what is meant by the term 'Course assessment'
- what is involved in your Performance
- what is involved in the reading/writing paper
- what is involved in the listening paper
- what is involved in the assignment – writing.

Be sure to make good use of this book and all your course materials while you prepare for your National 5 assessments – you have the skills and the tools necessary to succeed, and as long as you do your best you will achieve a grade of which you can be proud. Stay relaxed and focused – and, most of all, Viel Glück!

HOW DOES THE SQA ARRIVE AT YOUR FINAL GRADE?

Once you have competed all of your external assessments, each of the scaled marks you achieve will be added together, and the examiners will give you an overall mark out of 100 which will translate into your grade. The percentages for achieving each grade vary, but obviously the higher the better!

 ## THINGS TO DO AND THINK ABOUT

Top tips for tackling the exam:
- If possible, do some practice exam papers beforehand.
- Ensure you go to bed early the night before, having done all of your revision well in advance. If you are tired on the day, it will affect your performance.
- Ensure that your mobile phone is switched off and not kept in your pocket. If your phone goes off during the assessment, you could be asked to leave the room.
- Make sure you check that you have the right paper in front of you as soon as you sit down. Usually you will be given the correct one, but mistakes can be made so don't risk it!
- Read the introduction carefully and use the questions to help lead you to the answer.
- Only use the dictionary if absolutely necessary. The first word you see in the dictionary may not be the one you need, so do read all meanings and choose the one that makes the most sense.
- Use all the time given, and check your answers carefully. Remember, if they do not make sense to you, they will not make sense to the marker. Check your English too!

INTRODUCTION AND BULLET POINT 1

The aim of this section is to ensure you feel fully prepared for the writing section of the course assessment.

You will be revising some of the vocabulary and grammatical structures you have already seen in this book and will build on these to allow you to produce an accurate piece of writing that you feel comfortable with and are able to reproduce and adapt slightly on the day of your course assessment.

The writing part of the course assessment is worth a total of 20 marks (scaled to 15 marks) and will be 120–150 words in length. You may wish to write more, but remember that accuracy is key.

So, let's begin!

WHAT IS EXPECTED?

First of all, let's look at what you will be expected to write.

You will be expected to write an e-mail in response to a job advert. The job advert will be in German, advertising the job and giving other relevant details, such as the type of person you must be and whom to contact.

You will then have to write your e-mail based on the four predictable bullet points (these will always be the same) and the two less predictable bullet points (these will change from year to year, but will always be in the context of applying for the job).

Below is an example of the job advert and bullet points you will to have to address. The first four bullet points are the predictable ones and the remaining two the less predictable ones.

We will take each bullet point in turn.

> You are preparing an application for the job advertised below, and you write an e-mail in German to the company.
>
> > Wir suchen dringend mehrere Personen, die im Sommer bei uns als Kellner/in arbeiten wollen.
> >
> > Sie müssen motiviert sein und gute Kenntnisse in Englisch und Deutsch haben.
> >
> > Wenn Sie Interesse daran haben, schreiben Sie eine E-mail an Frau Hillert cafemozart@gmail.de.com
>
> To help you to write your e-mail, you have been given the following checklist of information to give about yourself. You must deal with all of these points:
>
> - personal details (name, age, where you live)
> - school/college education experience until now
> - skills/interests you have which make you right for the job
> - related work experience
> - when you will be available for interview and to work
> - any links to Germany or another German-speaking country.
>
> Use all of the above to help you write the e-mail in German, which should be 120–150 words. You may use a German dictionary.

BULLET POINT 1: PERSONAL DETAILS (NAME, AGE, WHERE YOU LIVE)

This should be a very straightforward start, as you will have seen and used these phrases in many other contexts. However, you must know how to spell these sentences correctly.

contd

For each piece of information required, we will provide A a basic approach and B a more advanced approach.

Name

A Ich heiße Bert Brown.
B Mein Vorname ist Bert und mein Familienname ist Brown.

Age

A Ich bin fünfzehn.
B Ich bin fünfzehn Jahre alt. Im Oktober werde ich sechzehn.

Where you live

A Ich wohne in Renfrew in Schottland.
B Ich wohne in Renfrew in der Nähe von Glasgow in Südwestschottland.

It is really important that you get off to a good start and ensure your basic German is accurate.

DON'T FORGET

Remember that the more information you can give accurately, then the better your chances of scoring a higher mark.

VIDEO LINK

Watch the clip at www. brightredbooks.net/ N5German for more on this.

ACTIVITY:

Look at the following examples and translate them into English.

Some words have been underlined so that you can adapt the passage to suit your needs.

Hallo, ich heiße <u>Thomas Fletcher</u> und ich bin <u>sechzehn</u> Jahre alt. Ich habe am <u>dritten September</u> Geburtstag. Ich wohne in <u>Thurso</u> in Nordostschottland. Thurso ist <u>eine kleine Stadt an der Küste</u> und es gibt ungefähr <u>10.000</u> Einwohner.

Mein Vorname ist <u>Julia</u> und mein Familienname ist <u>Brown</u>. Ich bin <u>fünfzehn</u> aber in zwei Wochen werde ich <u>sechzehn</u>. Ich wohne <u>in einem kleinen Dorf auf dem Land</u> nicht weit von Glasgow.

Ich heiße <u>Karolina Panasiuk</u> und am <u>achten Mai</u> werde ich <u>achtzehn</u> Jahre alt. Im Moment wohne ich in <u>Dumfries</u>, eine Stadt in Südschottland. Ich komme ursprünglich aus <u>Polen</u> aber ich wohne seit <u>zehn</u> Jahren in Schottland. Ich wohne gern in Schottland, weil die Landschaft so schön ist.

Mein Name ist <u>Craig Finlayson</u> und ich bin <u>siebzehn</u> Jahre alt. Ich wohne <u>in einer schönen Gegend in einem Vorort</u> von Aberdeen. Ich habe mein ganzes Leben hier gewohnt und die Gegend gefällt mir gut, weil es viel zu tun gibt und meine Freunde in der Nähe wohnen.

TOP TIPS

- Always write sentences that you feel comfortable with and that you can cope with when you have to learn them off by heart.
- Start learning each paragraph as you write it so you can reproduce it accurately on the day.

- Read your paragraph.
- Cover the first sentence and try to write it out.
- Check it.
- Repeat the process until you have written the whole paragraph accurately.

ONLINE TEST

Take the 'Writing: Introduction and personal details' test online at www.brightredbooks.net/ N5German

THINGS TO DO AND THINK ABOUT

Now it's your turn. Write a short paragraph on the first bullet point, including:

- your name
- your age
- where you live.

BULLET POINT 2: SCHOOL/COLLEGE EDUCATION EXPERIENCE UNTIL NOW

USEFUL PHRASES

Here are some possible phrases you could use:

- Ich besuche eine Schule, die (name of school) heißt.
- Ich bin in der elften Klasse.
- Dieses Jahr mache ich die National 5 Prüfungen.
- Die Pflichtfächer sind Mathe, Englisch und eine Fremdsprache. Ich habe Kunst, Chemie, Geschichte und Informatik gewählt.
- Meine Schule ist eine Gesamtschule und hat einen guten Ruf. Es gibt ungefähr tausend Schüler und Schülerinnen und achtzig Lehrer und Lehrerinnen.
- Meine Schule bietet eine gute Auswahl von Fächern und AGs.

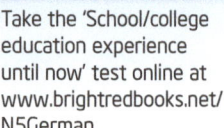

ONLINE TEST

Take the 'School/college education experience until now' test online at www.brightredbooks.net/N5German

SUBJECTS STUDIED LAST YEAR/SUBJECTS BEING STUDIED NOW

To avoid boring the marker and making too many mistakes, try not to list all the subjects you did last year and all the subjects you are doing this year. Here are some ways you could avoid this:

Letztes Jahr habe ich sechs Fächer aufs Niveau National 4 gelernt, einschließlich + (two subjects). Dieses Jahr lerne ich fünf Fächer aufs Niveau National 5.

Dieses Jahr mache ich die Prüfungen National 5 in sechs Fächern einschließlich + (two subjects). Nächstes Jahr werde ich Highers machen. Ich habe vier Fächer gewählt.

It is a good idea to use a range of tenses in your answer where possible: present, past and future.

SUBJECTS YOU LIKED/DIDN'T LIKE AND WHY/WHY NOT

Again, this should already be quite familiar to you, but it is always good to recap, so here are some expressions you could use to give your opinions and talk about subjects you like/dislike:

Opinions

Ich finde, dass Deutsch nützlich ist.
Meiner Meinung nach ist Deutsch nützlich.

Ich denke, dass Deutsch nützlich ist.
Ich glaube, dass Deutsch nützlich ist.

Subjects you like/dislike

Love/like

Ich liebe Geschichte
Ich mag Geschichte.
Ich lerne gern Geschichte.
Geschichte gefällt mir.
Ich interessiere mich für Geschichte.
Mein Lieblingsfach ist Geschichte.

Hate/dislike

Ich hasse Erdkunde.
Ich mag Erdkunde nicht.
Ich lerne nicht gern Erdkunde.
Erdkunde gefällt mir nicht.
Ich interessiere mich gar nicht für Erdkunde.
Ich kann Erdkunde nicht leiden.

NOTE: Meine Lieblingsfächer sind Musik und Theater.

Mein bestes Fach ist Geschichte.

Mein schlimmstes Fach ist Erdkunde

ACTIVITY: *Positiv* or *negativ*

Let's look more closely at what we could say about the subjects we like/dislike.

Put the phrases below under the headings *positiv* or *negativ*.

- Ich habe gute Noten in Mathe.
- Ich bin schwach in Chemie.
- Ich finde Biologie schwierig.
- Ich bekomme schlechte Noten in Informatik.
- Ich mache gute Fortschritte in Kunst.
- Ich finde Deutsch wichtig für meine Zukunft.
- Meiner Meinung nach ist Erdkunde einfach.

SCHOOL INVOLVEMENT

You could talk about any clubs, groups or teams that you are involved in. Here are some ideas to get you started:

- Ich bin im Chor/im Orchester in der Schule.
- Ich bin in der Volleyballmannschaft und wir trainieren zweimal in der Woche.
- Ich helfe mit der Freihandelgruppe/Umweltschutzgruppe.

FUTURE ASPIRATIONS

The second bullet point is probably the best place to add what you would like to do in the future.

- Nach der Schule werde ich mir eine Lehre suchen.
- Wenn ich gute Noten in den Prüfungen bekomme, werde ich zur Uni gehen.

Other ways of talking about the future:

- Ich hoffe, dass ich an der Uni studieren werde.
- Ich habe vor, an der Uni zu studieren.

If you do not have set plans, you can use the conditional tense.

- Ich würde gern ein Gap Jahr machen.

DON'T FORGET

Remember to use a variety of liking and disliking phrases and avoid repetition at all costs!

VIDEO LINK

For more on this, watch the clip at www.brightredbooks.net/N5German

THINGS TO DO AND THINK ABOUT

You are now ready and armed with all the phrases you need to write your second bullet point. To help you a little more and also to give you some listening practice, try to complete the following passage about school using the words given in the box below. Listen to the track online to hear the passage read aloud. For a bigger challenge, try not to look at the words.

Ich _____ eine Gesamtschule, die Clever High School _____. Die Schule ist sehr _____ und modern und es gibt _____tausend Schüler und Schülerinnen und achtzig _____. Die Schule hat einen guten _____. Ich gehe gern zur Schule, weil die Lehrer alles gut _____ und es viele AGs gibt.

_____ Jahr habe ich sieben Fächer für National 4 gemacht. Die _____ waren Englisch und Mathe. Dieses Jahr habe ich fünf Fächer. Ich _____ Informatik, weil es _____ für meine Zukunft ist. Meiner _____ nach ist eine Fremdsprache nützlich. Ich lerne nicht gern Physik, weil es _____ ist.

Nach der Schule _____ ich zur Uni gehen. Ich möchte Psychologie _____.

ungefähr   werde   schwierig   heißt   Meinung   Pflichtfächer   erklären   Ruf

groß   mag   besuche   studieren   letztes   wichtig   Lehrer

DON'T FORGET

Remember to think about German word-order rules.

VIDEO LINK

Watch the clip on future plans at www.brightredbooks.net/N5German

ONLINE TEST

Test yourself on this at www.brightredbooks.net/N5German

BULLET POINT 3: SKILLS/INTERESTS YOU HAVE WHICH MAKE YOU RIGHT FOR THE JOB

This bullet point allows you to write about any skills and/or interests you may have which make you the ideal candidate.

POSSIBLE WAYS OF STARTING

1 Ich habe die Anzeige in der Zeitung gesehen.
2 Ich möchte mich um die Stelle als … bewerben.
3 Ich habe die richtigen Eigenschaften für den Job.

It is important to know a range of adjectives for the qualities for different jobs:

Ich bin …

- fleißig
- freundlich
- kreativ
- pünktlich
- höflich
- verständnisvoll
- vertrauenswürdig
- geduldig

Personal qualities

- Ich spreche fließend Deutsch und Französisch.
- Ich habe gern Kontakt zu Menschen.
- Ich habe Teamgeist.
- Ich kann gut organiseren und gut zuhören.
- Ich kann unter Druck arbeiten.

Other reasons

- Ich möchte meine Fremdsprachen üben.
- Ich möchte meine Deutschkenntnisse verbessern.
- In der Zukunft möchte ich im Ausland arbeiten.
- Ich möchte eine neue Kultur kennen lernen.
- Ich möchte meine Berufserfahrungen erweitern.

SKILLS PHRASES FOR SPECIFIC JOBS

The phrases above are very general and could be used for any job. Below are some more phrases that are suited to specific jobs.

im Tourismusbereich

- Ich interessiere mich für einen Beruf im Tourismus.
- Ich arbeite gern in einem Team.
- Ich komme gut mit meinen Kollegen aus.
- Ich arbeite gern mit Menschen.

in einem Museum

- Ich interessiere mich für Kunst, Geschichte und Lernen.
- Ich möchte Arbeitserfahrung sammeln.

Kindergärtner/Kindergärtnerin

- Ich verstehe mich gut mit Kindern.
- Ich babysitte oft für die Kinder meiner Nachbarn.
- In der Schule helfe ich dem Sportlehrer mit der Volleyballmannschaft.
- Ich möchte gerne einen Beruf, wo ich mit Kindern arbeite.

auf einem Campingplatz

- Ich möchte draußen/im Freien arbeiten.
- Ich kann Spiele und Ausflüge organisieren.

INTERESTS RELEVANT TO THE JOB

This bullet point also asks you to mention any interests you have that may make you right for the job. Think carefully about this: watching TV or spending time talking to your friends on social media are probably not the interests most employers are looking for.

Again, as with bullet point 1, you will have a lot of phrases to talk about your interests. Here are just some ideas of how to make your sentences more interesting.

Possible ways of introducing interests

- In meiner Freizeit spiele ich Golf.
- Wenn ich Zeit habe, fahre ich Rad.
- Um mich zu entspannen, gehe ich wandern.
- Was ich gerne mache, ist Lesen.
- Meine Leidenschaft ist Schwimmen.
- Mein Lieblingshobby ist Leichtathletik.

Sport

- Ich bin sehr sportlich und ich gehe jeden Tag joggen. Meiner Meinung nach ist es wichtig fit und gesund zu bleiben.
- Ich bin Mitglied eines Segelvereins.
- Sport spielt eine wichtige Rolle in meinem Leben.
- Wenn das Wetter schön ist, mache ich einen Spaziergang.

Musik

- Um mich zu entspannen, höre ich Musik.
- Wenn ich gestresst bin, höre ich Musik.
- Ich spiele seit zwei Jahren Gitarre/Klavier.
- Ich schwärme für Musik, besonders klassische Musik.

Andere Interessen

- Ich gehe gern ins Kino, um die neuesten Filme zu sehen.
- Ich interessiere mich sehr für Geschichte und gehe oft ins Museum, um Austellungen zu besuchen.
- Ich bin sehr kreativ. Ich bastele gerne und ich male und zeichne auch.
- Ich kann stundenlang lesen, besonders Krimis.
- Dieses Jahr muss ich viel für die Prüfungen lernen und deshalb mache ich jeden Abend Hausaufgaben.

 ## THINGS TO DO AND THINK ABOUT

A bit of a challenge now: try to translate the following sentences into German. This is a difficult task, but use the phrases you have just learned to help you.

1. I saw the advert in the newspaper and I would like to apply for the job as waiter/waitress.
2. I would like to get to know a new culture and improve my German.
3. I am very hard-working and I like working in a team.
4. I have the right qualities for the job. I am polite and trustworthy.
5. When I leave school, I would like to work abroad and use my foreign languages.
6. In my free time, I love doing sport. I am in a hockey team and I train every Saturday.
7. When I have time, I love to go for a walk. It is important to stay fit and healthy.
8. I am very interested in music, and I have been learning to play the guitar for three years.
9. My passion is the cinema. I go once a week to the cinema.
10. When the weather is nice, I like to go horse-riding in the countryside.

 DON'T FORGET

Remember that you are applying for a job, and so try to keep your language as positive as possible. Make yourself sound interesting.

 VIDEO LINK

Watch the clip about leisure activities at www.brightredbooks.net/N5German

 ONLINE TEST

Head to www.brightredbooks.net/N5German to test yourself on this.

BULLET POINT 4: RELATED WORK EXPERIENCE

In this section, you will be required to write about any related work experience you may have. This could be about your work-experience week or a full-time/part-time job you may currently have.

QUICK REMINDER

Let's start with any work experience you may have done. You will need to use the perfect and imperfect tenses, so here is a quick reminder. Refer back to pp. 70–71 if you need more practice on these tenses.

Perfect tense

1 Present tense of *haben* or *sein*.
2 Past participle – take the infinitive, remove '-en' from the end and add 'ge-' to the front and '-t' to the end
3 Remember to learn the irregular verbs.

Imperfect tense

You can get away with just using *sein* in the imperfect tense, especially *war* and *waren*.

PAST WORK EXPERIENCE

Now we can start to write about past work experience.

Time phrases

- letztes Jahr
- vor einem Jahr
- während der Sommerferien

Where you worked

Ich habe in … gearbeitet   or   Ich habe mein Arbeitspraktikum in … gemacht.

- in einem Restaurant
- in einem Büro
- in einer Bibliothek
- in einem Supermarkt
- in einem Modegeschäft
- in einer Grundschule

or

Ich habe als … gearbeitet. (remember: no article before the job)

- Kellner/Kellnerin
- Mitarbeiter/Mitarbeiterin
- Zimmermädchen
- Kassierer/Kassiererin
- Verkäufer/Verkäuferin

⚙ ACTIVITY What you did – was du gemacht hast

Match the German phrases to the English.

Ich musste…

1 die Tische decken	A look after the children
2 die Tische abräumen	B play with the children
3 die Papiere sortieren	C set the tables
4 die Kunden bedienen	D welcome customers
5 auf die Kinder aufpassen	E clear the tables
6 das Telefon beantworten	F sort out the files
7 mit den Kindern spielen	G serve customers
8 die Bestellungen aufnehmen	H answer the phone
9 die Kunden begrüßen	I take orders

contd

What you thought of it

As you are applying for a job, you should try to make this a positive experience. Here are a few examples of some opinions you could give.

EXAMPLE

Das Arbeitspraktikum hat Spaß gemacht.

- Ich habe meinen ersten Einblick in die Arbeitswelt bekommen.
- Ich habe viel gelernt.
- Ich habe viele neue Leute kennengelernt.
- Ich habe mich sehr gut mit meinen Kollegen verstanden.
- Es war eine ausgezeichnete Erfahrung.
- Ich habe mein eigenes Geld verdient.

You can mix and match the reasons above, but remember to use the ones you feel most comfortable with and will be able to remember and reproduce accurately.

 **ACTIVITY:** Max's work experience

Listen to the audio track and answer the following questions.

1. When did Max do his work placement? (1)
2. Where did he work? (1)
3. What tasks did he do? Mention three things. (3)
4. How did he get on with the staff? (2)
5. What did he gain from doing the placement? Mention two things. (2)

Now it's your turn. Write a paragraph about any work experience and/or past job you have had.

CURRENT WORK

You may currently have a job and want to write about this. If you have a job at the moment, use the vocabulary you have just learned, but change to the present tense. The only real change for this part will be the time phrases:

- Im Moment arbeite ich in einem Supermarkt.
- Seit einem Jahr arbeite ich als Kellner(in) in einem Restaurant im Dorf.
- Während der Sommerferien arbeite ich als Zimmermädchen.
- Am Wochenende babysitte ich für die Nachbarn.

You are now ready to write about any job you currently have. Remember this will be in the present tense, but the vocabulary and phrases will remain the same.

 ## THINGS TO DO AND THINK ABOUT

You should now have written the first four predictable bullet points. These bullet points will always be part of the job application, and if you learn them well you should feel comfortable to reproduce what you have written in accurate German.

 DON'T FORGET

You can refer back to the employability section for more ideas on jobs.

 VIDEO LINK

Check out the clip at www.brightredbooks.net/N5German for more vocabulary on work experience.

 ONLINE TEST

Take the 'Related work experience' test online at www.brightredbooks.net/N5German

BULLET POINTS 5 AND 6: THE UNPREDICTABLE ONES

Now let's move onto the two unpredictable bullet points. These will change every year but will still relate to applying for a job. Don't forget the contexts and topics you will have already covered at National 5, as many of these could help you to complete these unpredictable points.

It would be impossible to try to cover every possibility in this book, but below are a few examples.

We will start with the examples given in the sample question paper at the beginning of this section.

WHEN YOU WILL BE AVAILABLE FOR INTERVIEW AND TO WORK?

- Ich kann im Juni zu einem Vorstellungsgespräch kommen.
- Ich kann im Juli und August arbeiten.

ANY LINKS TO GERMANY OR ANOTHER GERMAN-SPEAKING COUNTRY?

If asked to cover this bullet point, you may wish to talk about a past trip to a German-speaking country, or perhaps you visit a German-speaking country on a more regular basis as you have family or friends living there.

Here are a couple of examples to give you an idea of what you could write.

EXAMPLE:

Vor zwei Jahren bin ich für eine Woche in die Schweiz gefahren. Ich bin mit einer Schulgruppe dorthin gefahren und wir haben in einer Jugendherberge übernachtet. Die Reise hat viel Spaß gemacht und ich habe mein Deutsch verbessert. Ich möchte die Schweiz nochmal besuchen.

EXAMPLE:

Jedes Jahr verbringe ich die Sommerferien in Deutschland, weil meine Tante in einer Stadt in der Nähe von Hamburg wohnt. Wenn das Wetter schön ist, machen wir eine Radtour oder wir baden im See. Deutschland gefällt mir echt gut. Der Kuchen ist köstlich und der Kaffee schmeckt einfach besser. Ich rede gern auf Deutsch mit meinen Verwandten. Sie korrigieren mich, wenn ich Fehler mache.

OTHER POSSIBILITIES

1 Experience of travel

EXAMPLE:

Ich reise gern, um eine neue Kultur kennen zu lernen. Man erweitert den Horizont und man wird toleranter. Ich habe Spanien und Griechenland schon besucht. Ich interessiere mich sehr für die Kultur/das Essen/die Sprache.

2 Relevance to future plans

EXAMPLE:

Ich möchte an der Uni studieren und ich brauche Geld für mein Studium. Ich werde selbstständiger werden. Ich möchte meine Fremdsprachen verbessern. Ich möchte später im Ausland arbeiten.

contd

3 How you can contribute to the company/hotel

EXAMPLE

Ich kann mit der Verwaltung helfen. Ich kann aufräumen und putzen. Ich kann das Telefon beantworten und E-mails schreiben. Ich kann den Kunden helfen.

4 Why you are interested in the job

EXAMPLE

Ich möchte im Ausland arbeiten und mein Deutsch verbessern. Ich möchte Arbeitserfahrung sammeln. Ich möchte mein Selbstvertrauen entwickeln. Ich möchte eine andere Kultur kennen lernen.

5 Languages spoken

EXAMPLE

Ich spreche fließend Englisch. Ich habe gute Deutschkenntnisse. Ich lerne seit vier Jahren Deutsch.

6 Questions about the job

EXAMPLE

Muss ich eine Uniform tragen?   Was sind die Arbeitsstunden?

Wie viel Geld verdiene ich pro Stunde?   Welchen Tag habe ich frei?

You should now have a complete piece of writing.

TOP TIPS

- Always read the job advert thoroughly and apply for the job that is being advertised.
- Write in paragraphs – this will ensure you cover all the bullet points and make it easier for the marker to check your work.
- Write neatly. Markers have to mark a lot of papers, and it is very important that they can read your handwriting.
- The first four bullet points will always be the same, so learn these very thoroughly.
- Learn how to spell *ich heiße*, and remember that *Jahre* is written with a capital letter. Get off to a good start.
- Be careful when talking about your subjects. Make sure you spell them correctly.
- When writing about a job, do not use the word for 'a': *Ich arbeite als Kellner/Kellnerin*.
- For the final two bullet points, which are less predictable, make sure your German is accurate. Your teacher or lecturer will have covered many possibilities with you, so try to learn these.
- Be careful when asking questions. Try to use a question word and think about the word-order rules.
- Remember always to read over your work at the end. Check the following:
  - Does it make sense?
  - Have I covered all the bullet points?
  - Is my spelling accurate?
  - Have I used my accents correctly?
  - Are my tenses accurate?
  - Finally, only use the dictionary to check spelling/genders/accents. Do not try to translate phrases in your head from English to German.

DON'T FORGET

You can refer to the section on Holidays for more ideas about travel.

VIDEO LINK

For more on this, watch the clip at www.brightredbooks.net/N5German

ONLINE TEST

Take the 'Unpredictable bullet points' test online at www.brightredbooks.net/N5German

THINGS TO DO AND THINK ABOUT

- Make sure your German is accurate – know your grammar points.
- To help you learn, read a line, close your notebook and write it out again.
- Check over your work.
- Change any sentences/phrases you find difficult to remember.
- Only use a dictionary to check spelling. Do not start making up sentences on the day.

APPENDICES

TRANSCRIPTS

LEARNING

Describing my school – Meine Schule beschreiben
 ACTIVITY Tobias's school

Ich heiße Tobias. Ich besuche eine Gesamtschule. Die Schule liegt in einem Dorf nicht weit von meinem Haus. Die Plichtfächer sind Mathe, Deutsch und eine Fremdsprache. Ich habe Chemie, Geschichte, Werken und Sport gewählt. Mein Lieblingsfach ist Sport, weil es Spaß macht. Der Lehrer ist verständnisvoll. Ich finde Geschichte furchtbar. Wir müssen so viel schreiben. Chemie ist wichtig für meine Zukunft. Ich möchte Medizin an der Universität studieren.

Das Gebäude ist ein bißchen altmodisch und viele Klassenzimmer sind sehr klein aber ordentlich. Es gibt einen ausgezeichneten Sportplatz, wo man Fußball spielen kann. Die Bibliothek hat eine gute Auswahl an Büchern. Ich bin Mitglied des Schachklubs. Wir haben die letzten vier Spiele gewonnen.

EMPLOYABILITY

Part-time jobs – Teilzeitjobs 2
 ACTIVITY Peter's part-time job

Ich habe einen Teilzeitjob. Ich brauche das Geld für meinen Urlaub in Griechenland. Nach der Abiturprüfung wollen meine Freunde und ich in den Urlaub fahren. Ich habe einen Job als Kellner in einem italienischen Café im Dorf gefunden. Ich arbeite den ganzen Tag am Samstag und am Sonntagnachmittag. Der Job gefällt mir gut, weil ich gern Kontakt zu Menschen habe. Ich bin gesellig und lustig. Der Job kann manchmal anstrengend sein, besonders im Sommer, wenn das Wetter so heiß ist. Aber es passiert auch, dass einige Kunden schlecht gelaunt sind und nicht besonders freundlich sind. Das finde ich schwierig, das muss ich zugeben. Was ich am besten mag, ist dass ich acht Euro pro Stunde bekomme und noch Trinkgeld dazu. Die Arbeit ist ganz gut bezahlt. Ich wohne in der Nähe von dem Café und kann zu Fuß zur Arbeit gehen. Ich finde einen Nebenjob eine gute Idee. Man wird selbstständiger und man entwickelt sein Selbstvertrauen. Man bekommt auch einen Einblick in die Arbeitswelt.

CULTURE

Holidays – Die Ferien 1
 ACTIVITY Heike's holidays

Jedes Jahr fahren wir im Herbst in den Urlaub. Wir fahren auf Teneriffa an die Küste. Ferien am Strand finde ich toll. Ich mag das sommerliche Wetter. Wir mieten eine Ferienwohnung mit Schwimmbecken und Blick aufs Meer. Wir frühstücken draußen auf der Terrasse. Tagsüber gehen wir an den Strand zum Sonnenbaden. Wir haben Verwandte, die ein Haus auf Teneriffa gekauft haben. Abends treffen wir uns zum Essen. Wir gehen in eine Gaststätte und probieren die Spezialitäten – normalerweise Meeresfrüchte.

contd

Meine Eltern sagen, dass ich zu jung bin mit Freunden in den Urlaub zu fahren. Ich möchte so gerne unabhängig sein und mit Freunden wegfahren. Dann können wir machen, was wir wollen. Ein Vorteil ist, dass meine Eltern alles bezahlen. Ein Nachteil ist, dass ich wenig Freiheit habe und es viele Regeln gibt. Meine Eltern wollen immer wissen, wohin ich gehe und mit wem. Ich muss um Mitternacht zurückkommen. Das ist peinlich!

Mein Traumurlaub wäre mit meiner besten Freundin Gabi in den Urlaub zu fahren. Wir verstehen uns sehr gut. Wir haben die gleichen Interessen und den gleichen Geschmack und Gabi bringt mich immer zum Lachen. Ich möchte gerne nach Griechenland fahren und etwas Neues entdecken. Wir würden jeden Abend in Nachtlokale gehen und am nächsten Morgen bis Mittag ausschlafen. Meine Eltern wollen immer die Sehenswürdigkeiten besichtigen oder eine Stadtrundfahrt machen. Das ist viel zu anstrengend.

COURSE ASSESSMENT: WRITING

Bullet point 4: Related work experience

 ACTIVITY: Max's work experience

Ich habe mein Arbeitspraktikum im Februar gemacht. Ich habe in einer Grundschule gearbeitet. Ich habe fünf Tage dort verbracht. Ich habe mit den Kindern gespielt. Ich habe die Hefte korrigiert. Ich habe im Sportunterricht mitgemacht. An einem Tag haben wir eine Wanderung im Wald gemacht. Ich bin sehr gut mit meinen Kollegen ausgekommen. Die Chefin war hilfsbereit und verständnisvoll. Ich habe viel gelernt. Ich habe mein Selbstvertrauen entwickelt und ich habe den ersten Einblick in die Arbeitswelt bekommen. Ich würde ein Arbeitspraktikum empfehlen.

ANSWERS

SOCIETY

Family and friends – Familie und Freunde 1

 **ACTIVITY** Hast du Geschwister? – Do you have any brothers or sisters?

1 stepbrother
2 half-sister
3 younger brother
4 older sister
5 twin brother
6 adopted sister

 **ACTIVITY** Quiz: Wer ist das?

1 der Onkel
2 die Schwester
3 der Cousin
4 die Tante
5 der Neffe
6 die Oma

 **ACTIVITY** Translation

1 My stepbrother is married with three children.
2 My sister is single.
3 My Grandpa is dead.
4 My stepsister and her husband are separated.
5 My cousin is engaged.
6 My uncle and (my) aunt are divorced.

ACTIVITY New type of family

1 When the child lives with one parent (Mum and child/Dad and child).
2 One family out of four.
3 • There are so many problems at home.
   • One of the parents may have lost his/her job.
   • There are money/financial problems.
   • The parents don't love each other any more.
   • They have other interests.
4 • There is not enough space in the house.
   • The parents don't have enough time for all the children.

THINGS TO DO AND THINK ABOUT

einen
Er
Sein
Seine
Meine
Ihr
Sie
Meine
Sie

Meine
Sie
ihre
Der
Er
Sein

Family and friends – Familie und Freunde 2

ACTIVITY Match up

1 E
2 G
3 I
4 F
5 A
6 C
7 B
8 J
9 H
10 D

ACTIVITY *Richtig* or *falsch*?

1 Falsch
2 Richtig
3 Falsch
4 Richtig
5 Richtig
6 Falsch
7 Richtig
8 Falsch
9 Richtig
10 Falsch
11 Richtig
12 Falsch

ACTIVITY Translation

1 My Gran is very hard-working and her house is always tidy.
2 My brother is especially sociable and he has a large circle of friends.
3 My aunt is understanding and sympathetic and she listens to my problems.
4 My stepbrother is lazy and never helps in the house.
5 My cousin is annoying because she must talk the whole time.
6 My Grandpa is always funny and likes to tell jokes.
7 My Mum is mostly good-natured because she always thinks positively.
8 My uncle is creative and imaginative and organises trips for us.

THINGS TO DO AND THINK ABOUT

1 a oft
   b nie
   c immer
   d manchmal
2 a wirklich
   b sehr

   c   ganz

   d   echt

3 a   lustig

   b   freundlich

   c   geduldig

Relationships – Die Beziehungen

 **ACTIVITY** Match up

1 C

2 E

3 G

4 H

5 A

6 K

7 I

8 B

9 J

10 D

11 F

ACTIVITY Complete each sentence

1 geben

2 haben

3 hilft

4 hat

5 gibt

6 helfen

7 haben

8 haben

Family conflicts – Streit mit der Familie

ACTIVITY *Richtig* or *falsch*?

Translations:

1 My parents are very strict.

2 They treat me like a child.

3 My parents have no time for me.

4 My parents don't understand me.

5 They have old-fashioned ideas.

6 My parents criticise my clothes and friends.

ACTIVITY 'Weil' clauses

1 Ich komme gut mit meiner Mutter aus, weil sie geduldig und tolerant ist.

2 Ich mag meinen Bruder nicht, weil er mir auf die Nerven geht.

3 Ich verstehe mich gut mit meinem Vater, weil er mir mit den Hausaufgaben hilft.

4 Ich habe ein gutes Verhältnis zu meiner Oma, weil sie immer Zeit für mich hat.

5 Ich komme gut mit meinen Eltern aus, weil wir die gleichen Interessen haben.

6 Ich mag meine Eltern nicht, weil sie meine Kleidung kritisieren.

7 Ich verstehe mich gut mit meinen Eltern, weil sie mir viel Freiheit geben.

8 Ich verstehe mich nicht gut mit meinen Eltern, weil ich wenig Taschengeld bekomme.

ACTIVITY Match up

1 C

2 D

3 A

4 G

5 F

6 H

7 E

8 B

ACTIVITY Arguing with parents

1 Pocket money/housework/homework

2 Going out

3 Go out on Saturday night until midnight/go on holiday with friends

4 When the child does not tidy his/her bedroom or gets bad marks at school

5 Cheeky and lazy

House rules – Hausregeln

ACTIVITY Rules

a 1 I am not allowed to have a party.

    2 I am not allowed to eat sweets.

    3 I am not allowed to watch TV.

    4 I am not allowed to play computer games.

    5 I am not allowed to eat fast food.

    6 I am not allowed to go to the disco.

    7 I am not allowed to phone my friends.

    8 I am not allowed to go into town on my own.

    9 I am not allowed to have a piercing.

    10 I am not allowed to smoke.

    11 I am not allowed to drink alcohol.

    12 I am not allowed to dye my hair.

    13 I am not allowed to buy clothes myself.

    14 I am not allowed to take drugs.

b 1 I must tidy my room.

    2 I must do my homework.

    3 I must help out in the house.

    4 I must wash the car.

    5 I must cook dinner.

    6 I must feed the dog.

    7 I must look after my little brother.

    8 I must visit my Gran.

ACTIVITY Sind deine Eltern streng? Gibt es Regeln?

1 Ich darf (nicht) in die Disko gehen.

2 Ich darf (nicht) fernsehen.

3 Ich darf (nicht) rauchen.

4 Ich darf (keinen) Alkohol trinken.

5 Ich darf ein (kein) Piercing haben.

6 Ich darf eine (keine) Party geben.

7 Ich darf (nicht) allein in die Stadt gehen.

8 Ich darf (kein) Fastfood essen.

9 Ich darf (nicht) bei Freunden übernachten.

 **ACTIVITY** Missing words

bei

interessieren

Schule

übernachten

abends

Angst

elf

Konflikte

Urlaub

Ideal parents and people who influence me – Ideale Eltern und Leute, die mich beeinflussen

ACTIVITY Ideal parents

1 Ideal parents would be patient and tolerant.

2 Ideal parents would help me with my homework.

3 Ideal parents would give me lots of freedom.

4 Ideal parents would have no house rules.

5 Ideal parents would have modern ideas.

6 Ideal parents would have time for their children.

7 Ideal parents would not criticise their children.

8 Ideal parents would accept my friends.

9 Ideal parents would not have a favourite child.

10 Ideal parents would give lots of pocket money.

ACTIVITY Conditional tense

1 Ich würde mit meinen Kindern reden.

2 Ich würde viel Zeit mit meinen Kindern verbringen.

3 Ich würde interessante Aktivitäten für meine Kinder planen.

4 Ich würde meine Kinder ermutigen.

5 Ich würde meinen Kindern Ratschläge geben.

ACTIVITY What makes a good parent?

Julia

Good parents make their children happy.

Happy children are normally healthy and full of energy.

Good parents set achievable goals.

Maximilian

Good parents respect their child's personality.

They accept all children are different.

You can point out your child's strengths and weaknesses but concentrate on the strengths.

Moritz

Good parents do lots of things with their child.

They talk to him/her every day.

They help him/her with homework.

ACTIVITY Grandparents

1 More and more mothers are going back to work after having a baby.

The dad works all day.

Childcare is expensive.

2 One third of all children under the age of six stay with their grandparents once a week.

3 Grandparents are often not so strict and they spoil the children.

4 The children are allowed to eat more sweets or go to bed later.

5 The dad was cheeky as a child or the mum did not get good marks at school.

Housework - Hausarbeit

ACTIVITY Household chores

Ich koche

Ich mähe den Rasen

Ich sauge Staub

Ich räume mein Zimmer auf

Ich wasche ab

Ich gehe mit dem Hund spazieren

Ich wasche das Auto

Ich mache mein Bett

Ich arbeite im Garten

Ich gehe einkaufen

Ich gieße die Blumen

Ich decke den Tisch

Ich wasche die Kleider

Ich bügele

ACTIVITY Sentence-builder

Possible answers:

1 Ich räume ab und zu mein Zimmer auf.

2 Ich mache nie mein Bett.

3 Ich decke manchmal den Tisch.

4 Ich bügele jeden Tag.

 **ACTIVITY** Housework survey

1 Almost half of the pupils help <u>now and again at the weekend</u>. <u>About a quarter</u> help on a weekday for roughly half an hour.

2 Tidying bedroom/making beds

3 Half an hour

4 When you don't get pocket money or you have to help out a lot in the house.

Friendship - Freundschaft

ACTIVITY Match up 1

1 E

2 I

3 A

4 G

5 J

6 B

7   H
8   C
9   D
10 F

 **ACTIVITY:** Sentence-builder

Possible answers:

1   immer
2   meistens
3   wirklich
4   sehr
5   Sport/Musik
6   Fußball/Geld

 **ACTIVITY:** Match up 2

hat immer Zeit für mich	has always got time for me
hat viel Geduld	has lots of patience
redet mit mir über alles	talks to me about everything
gibt immer Unterstützung	is always supportive
hat die gleichen Interessen	has the same interests
hilft mir, wenn ich Probleme habe	helps me when I have problems
ist hilfsbereit und vertrauenswürdig	is helpful and understanding
hält zu mir	sticks by me

 **ACTIVITY:** Jan's friends

1   funny and friendly
2   both love tennis
    they are in a club and train every Saturday
    they talk about music and computer games
3   the friend is lazy and unpunctual
    the friend causes him to be late for school
    he copies his homework

 **ACTIVITY:** Was ist deine Meinung?

1   There is sometimes peer pressure.
2   You must be in the gang.
3   You must wear designer clothes and drink alcohol.
4   You must behave badly to get the respect of the others.
5   You must smoke to be fashionable and cool.
6   It is difficult to stand up against the group.

Leisure – Die Freizeit

 ACTIVITY: Match up the instruments

1   C
2   E
3   G
4   F
5   D
6   B
7   A

 **ACTIVITY:** Hobby phrases

1   I watch TV.
2   I read magazines/books/newspapers.
3   I listen to music/the radio.
4   I do sport.
5   I laze about.
6   I go on my bike/cycle.
7   I cook.
8   I visit my gran.
9   I wander round the town.
10 I do my homework.
11 I knit.
12 I do craftwork.
13 I paint.
14 I draw.

Television – Das Fernsehen

 **ACTIVITY:** What programme?

1   Zeichentrickfilme
2   Krimis
3   Abenteuerfilme
4   die Nachrichten
5   Komödien
6   Liebesfilme
7   Werbung
8   Sportsendungen
9   Seifenopern
10 Musiksendungen
11 Spielshows
12 Kriegsfilme
13 Natursendungen
14 die Wettervorhersage
15 Gruselfilme

 **ACTIVITY:** For or against TV

1   für   TV is an important source of information.
2   gegen   There are too many adverts.
3   gegen   Too many programmes are stupid.
4   für   You learn about what is happening in the world.
5   für   You can relax.
6   gegen   Children watch hours of TV. They are too passive.
7   für   You can learn about another culture.
8   für   You can talk about the programmes. It is sociable.
9   gegen   There is too much violence and brutality.
10 für   You can forget about daily life.
11 gegen   TV is like a drug. You quickly become addicted.
12 gegen   You hear lots of swear words.

Is TV good or bad for us? – Ist das Fernsehen gut oder schlecht für uns?

⚙ ACTIVITY Fill in the blanks

Lea

viel

Nachrichten

Welt

Kultur

Justin

Gewalt

Kinder

dick

Familien

Felix

meistens

entspannen

Alltag

Lina

blöde

todlangweilig

Schimpfwörter

Blut

⚙ ACTIVITY Florian und Melanie sprechen über Reality TV

1 It was so funny/he laughed so much. (2)

2 *Any two from:* Can't stand them/can't believe how popular the shows are/they are pointless/they have nothing to do with real life. (2)

3 They are on every channel. (1)

4 *Any two from:* It is a competition/people want to earn a lot of money/people want to become famous/people want to fulfil their dream/people want to become famous singers. (2)

5 The contestants carry out shocking and embarrassing activities. (1)

6 It has a bad influence on young people/they think that they don't need to work at school/they can become rich quickly by going on one of these shows. (3)

7 A documentary (film) about people who do something for society. (1)

8 *Any two from:* He likes to observe other people's lives/how they interact with each other/you can learn a lot about humanity/it gives him hope that one day he can change his life. (2)

⚙ ACTIVITY Big Brother contestants

Name	What they liked	What they did not like
Jonas	Got on well with the other house contestants	He was lonely from time to time
Philipp	Having a long lie	Having to cook for himself
Alina	Family could watch her every night on TV	Missed her friends

Technology – die Technologie

⚙ ACTIVITY The dangers of the internet

- The information is not always correct, for example on Wikipedia.
- There are lots of viruses. Viruses damage the computer.
- The Internet is a forum for violence and pornography.
- Cyberbullying is a big problem.
- There are people who write a false profile and upload nasty photos.
- There are many hackers.
- Data theft is a problem.
- Paedophiles use the internet. They give a false name and age and chat like a friend.

Safety tips

- You should only write your profile for family and friends.
- You should use a nickname in chatrooms.
- You should not upload silly pictures of yourself.
- You should not give out contact details, especially your address and phone number.

⚙ ACTIVITY Survey about mobile phones

Frage 1

a 5% use their mobile very little

b 80% use their mobile constantly

c 1% never use their mobile

Frage 2

a 20% mostly use their mobile to download ringtones

b 27% mostly use their mobile to phone friends

c 12% mostly use their mobile to upload photos

d 23% mostly use their mobile to text

e 4% mostly use their mobile to get information

⚙ ACTIVITY Das Handy: pro oder kontra?

1 ✓ It is good for safety when you go walking in the mountains.

2 ✗ The mobile phone is like a drug.

3 ✓ My parents can always contact me.

4 ✗ Some people use their mobile phone while driving. That is dangerous.

5 ✗ A mobile phone rings in class. It disturbs the lesson.

6 ✓ It is important in an emergency – for example when your car breaks down on the motorway.

7 ✗ Some people text constantly.

8 ✗ The bill is always very high.

9 ✓ A mobile phone is more than just a phone. My mobile is a TV, camera and personal organiser.

10 ✗ Some people speak very loudly on their mobile phones.

11 ✗ The antenna masts are awful.

12 ✓ If the bus does not arrive, I can quickly phone my parents.

13 ✓ My mobile is also my computer. I can surf the internet and send e-mails.

Doing sport – Sport treiben

⚙ ACTIVITY Warum treibt man Sport? – Why do people do sport?

1 It is healthy.
2 You look younger.
3 It is fun.
4 You feel fit and well.
5 You are not ill as much.
6 You have more stamina and energy.
7 You have a slim figure.
8 You are more self-confident.
9 You can make new friends.
10 It is a break from everyday stress.
11 It is sociable.
12 You learn about team spirit.

⚙ ACTIVITY Fill in the blanks

1 spiele
2 gehe
3 gehe
4 mache
5 gehe
6 mache
7 spiele
8 mache

⚙ ACTIVITY When and how often do you do sport?

1 On Saturday mornings
2 On Friday evenings
3 Every day
4 Twice a week
5 At the weekend
6 In the holidays
7 On Thursday afternoons
8 After school
9 Once a week
10 Every Wednesday

⚙ ACTIVITY Who do you play with?

1 meinem
2 meiner
3 meinen
4 meiner
5 meinem
6 meinen
7 meinem
8 meiner

⚙ ACTIVITY Where do you play?

1 At the seaside
2 In the gym/sports hall
3 At the youth club
4 In the country
5 At the sports field
6 In the indoor pool
7 At the lake
8 In the gym

⚙ ACTIVITY Building sentences

1 Ich gehe am Samstag mit meinen Freunden auf dem Land reiten.
2 Ich gehe am Donnerstagabend mit meinem Vater im Sportzentrum schwimmen.
3 Ich gehe am Wochenende mit meinen Eltern am See segeln.

Health – Die Gesundheit

⚙ ACTIVITY Healthy and unhealthy food

Gesund = healthy
Seelachs = salmon
Apfelsaft = apple juice
Schinken = ham
Gemüse = vegetables
Vollkornbrot = wholemeal bread
Obst = fruit
Gulasch = stew
Reis = rice
Wasser = water
Hähnchen = chicken

Ungesund = unhealthy
Süßigkeiten = sweets
Chips = crisps
Frikadellen = meatballs
Pommes = chips
Käse = cheese
Schaschlik = kebab
Torte = cake
Bratkartoffeln = fried potatoes

⚙ ACTIVITY Eating habits

1 Nein – I eat nothing for breakfast.
2 Ja – I eat an apple at interval.
3 Nein – I like eating sweet stuff. I have a sweet tooth.
4 Ja – For lunch I have a ham sandwich with salad.
5 Nein – When I am hungry I eat crisps.
6 Ja – I drink eight glasses of water a day.
7 Nein – I eat a lot of frozen foods.
8 Ja – I avoid fatty foods.
9 Nein – For breakfast I eat a bar of chocolate.
10 Ja – When I am hungry I eat a banana.
11 Ja – I buy organic food.
12 Ja – For dinner I eat fish with rice.
13 Nein – I eat sweets at interval.
14 Ja – I never eat between meals.
15 Nein – I only drink lemonade or cola.
16 Ja – I eat five portions of fruit and vegetables a day.

17 Nein – For dinner I eat fried sausage with fried potatoes.

18 Nein – For lunch I eat a hamburger with chips.

19 Ja – I eat mainly wholemeal bread.

20 Nein – I often go to the snack bar.

 **ACTIVITY** Das Frühstück ist wichtig

Leaflet 1:

1 About one third

2 It is the most important meal of the day

3 It is regenerating

4 Productivity and keeping a slim figure

5 Carbohydrates – wholemeal products and muesli (cereal)
   Fibre – fruit and vegetables
   Protein-rich foods – ham, cheese, milk

6 It affects blood sugar levels, leading to a drop in performance or productivity/ravenous appetite

Leaflet 2:

1 Eat five meals throughout the day so you don't get a ravenous appetite.

2 It would be great to eat five portions of fruit and vegetables a day, either as a snack or with the main meal. They are good for vitamins and minerals.

3 Drink lots – 1.5 litres of liquid throughout the day, preferably water or diluted fruit juice.

4 Milk and dairy products are generally healthy as they contain calcium – check that the products have not been sweetened and are made from skimmed milk.

5 Only eat meat and sausage in small amounts. Fish is healthier and should be eaten once a week.

6 Try not to eat much sweet stuff. A bar of chocolate is allowed from time to time as long as it does not replace a meal when you are really hungry. Jelly bears (sweets) contain less fat than chocolate.

Do you have a healthy lifestyle? – Lebst du gesund?

ACTIVITY Leading a healthy lifestyle

1 Lukas

2 Lara

3 Felix

4 Thomas

5 Christina

6 Leon

7 Florian

8 Moritz

9 Luca

10 Michael

11 Gabi

12 David

13 Paul

14 Julia

15 Lisa

16 Lena

ACTIVITY Different lifestyles

Oliver

1 He has no time. (1)

2 When he was younger. (1)

3 Fatty foods and sweets. (2)

4 Avoid fast foods/eat more fruit and vegetables. (2)

5 A gym has opened up nearby.

Sabina

1 She leads a healthy lifestyle. (1)

2 Healthy eating is just as important as exercise. (1)

3 To forget her worries/to relax. (2)

4 She is supple/she has a different outlook on things. (2)

5 *Any two from:* She is not keen on fast food/she watches what she eats/when she is hungry she eats a low-fat yoghurt/she always has fruit with her. (2)

Hans

1 It is best to have a combination of the right food and exercise (2)

2 Running (1)

3 Fat (1)

4 He eats a lot of chicken and fish./He eats five portions of fruit and vegetables a day. (2)

5 He misses sweets and chocolate. (1)

Teenage addictions – Jugendsucht

ACTIVITY Opinions on smoking

1 I find smoking dangerous.

2 I find smoking awful.

3 I find smoking unhealthy.

4 I find smoking disgusting.

5 I find smoking unsociable.

6 I find smoking selfish.

ACTIVITY The physical effects of smoking

1 Smoking causes lung cancer

2 A cough

3 Breathing problems

4 Heart disease

5 Yellow skin

6 Bad breath

ACTIVITY For or against?

1 I smoke because it is relaxing.

2 I smoke because I get bad marks at school.

3 I don't drink alcohol because my friends are often drunk. They do and say stupid things.

4 I don't smoke as it kills you.

5 I smoke because it is fashionable.

6 I drink alcohol to forget my worries.

7 I smoke because I can't give up.

8 I smoke because I need to lose weight.

9 I drink alcohol to get rid of my inhibitions.

10 I smoke because it is sociable.

11 I don't smoke because you quickly become addicted.

12 I drink alcohol to be one of the gang.

13 When I smoke I have more self-confidence.

14 I don't smoke as lots of people die from lung cancer.

ACTIVITY Das Rauchen

1 As a teenager (1)

2 To combat stress (1)

3 You quickly become addicted/you can't give up (1)

4 *Any two from*: It causes lots of illnesses/it can cause lung cancer/it can kill/it contains dangerous substances such as nicotine and tar (2)

5 Peer pressure/no-one wants to be excluded/you need to belong to the group

ACTIVITY Der Alkoholismus

1 Liver/kidney/brain damage. (1)

2 It can lead to heavy shaking/and hallucinations. (2)

ACTIVITY Jugendliche und Drogen

1 It starts during school and ends at the start of adult life. (2)

2 Teenagers think that drugs are trendy/they ignore the dangers and enjoy the effects. (2)

3 *Any three answers:* You can relax (chill)/you can dance all night/you have fewer inhibitions/it is easier to get to know people. (3)

4 Drugs are bad for the heart and the liver. They can cause blood disease.

My home – Mein Zuhause

ACTIVITY Buildings

1 Semi-detached house

2 Detached house

3 Terraced house

4 Block of flats

5 High-rise flats

6 Flat

7 Farmhouse

8 Block of flats

ACTIVITY Where is your house?

1 In a village

2 In a town

3 In the mountains

4 In the country

5 In a suburb

6 At the seaside

7 In a city

8 On the coast

9 On the outskirts of town

10 In the town centre

ACTIVITY What is it like?

1 Tiny but bright

2 Dark and old-fashioned

3 Huge but family-friendly

4 Pretty and well looked after

5 Roomy and cosy

6 Tidy and comfortable

7 Untidy and dirty

8 Clean and charming

ACTIVITY Rooms

1 Basement – games room and utility room

2 Ground floor – living room, dining room, kitchen and toilet

3 First floor – three bedrooms, bathroom and guest room.

4 Attic – study

ACTIVITY Meine Gegend

1 On the border with France

2 On the east coast

3 In the Black Forest

4 On the river Rhine

5 It is the capital of Germany

6 On the Baltic Sea

7 Near Lake Constance

8 In Bavaria

9 On the river Danube

10 Vienna, the capital of Austria

My town – Mein Stadt

ACTIVITY Adjectives

Positive

schön	pretty
sauber	clean
ruhig	quiet
lebendig	lively
historisch	historical
hübsch	pretty
wunderbar	wonderful
umweltfreundlich	environmentally friendly
gut gepflegt	well looked after
sicher	safe

Negative

langweilig	boring
schmutzig	dirty
uralt	ancient
häßlich	ugly
lautnoisy	
deprimierend	depressing
verschmutzt	polluted
gefährlich	dangerous

ACTIVITY Why are these towns famous?

1 walking paths

2 football team

3 churches

4 music festival

APPENDICES

5   old houses
6   tourist attractions
7   shopping centre
8   white-water rafting
9   mountains
10   TV tower

 **ACTIVITY** Where I live

Matthias – pretty village on the coast – in the summer tourists visit the village from all over the world – you can go for a walk along the beach – go for a wander round town to look at the historical buildings – for those people who like water sports there is a choice of activities – you can go sailing or windsurfing – fishing is also a possibility – you can go on a boat trip and visit a small island.

Kerstin – lives in the city – there are lots of parks that are well looked after with lots of trees and flower beds – there is lots to do and see – you can buy a day ticket and travel around by underground and look at the tourist attractions – the city tour is worthwhile – the town has lots of entertainment: museums, art galleries, cinemas and bowling alleys – there is accommodation at all price levels – from luxury hotel to campsite or youth hostel.

 **ACTIVITY** Düsseldorf

A tourist town – Eine Touristenstadt

1   It is a former fishing village which lies on the river Düssel.
2   The airport is the third biggest in Germany.
3   From all the big European cities you can reach Düsseldorf in an hour.
4   Düsseldorf hosts over 40 international conferences a year.
5   The town is alive with 260 wine bars, pubs, breweries and cafés.
6   The old town is picturesque with narrow, cobbled streets.
7   You can stroll along the banks of the river Rhine.
8   Düsseldorf is a fashion town – along King Avenue you can find international brands.
9   Guided tours – whether on foot, by bus or boat – offer an overview of the town and provide an informative and entertaining experience.
10   Green is a dominant colour in Düsseldorf. Almost a fifth of the ground is for parks and forests. Düsseldorf is known as the garden city.

 **ACTIVITY** Home towns

Südwesten

lebendig

schmutzig

an der Küste

ruhig

bekannt

Bergen

Nordosten

hübsch

das Schloss

 **ACTIVITY** Buildings

das Krankenhaus – hospital

die Kirche – church

der Bahnhof – station
die Bibliothek – library
das Hallenbad – indoor pool
der Dom – cathedral
der Hafen – harbour
der Tierpark – zoo
das Freibad – outdoor pool
das Kino – cinema
das Schloss – castle
das Rathaus – town hall
die Fußgängerzone – pedestrian area

ACTIVITY Adjectives

1   hübsch**e**
2   neu**en**
3   interessant**es**
4   toll**en**
5   alt**es**

Town and country – Stadt und Land

ACTIVITY Advantages and disadvantages

1   a   There is lots to do for young people.
    b   The nightlife is great.
    c   It is lively.
    d   There is lots going on.
    e   There are lots of shopping facilities and entertainment facilities.
    f   There is a good choice of shops and pubs.
    g   The transport service is great.
    h   The shops are open 24 hours.
2   a   There is too much traffic.
    b   You can never find a parking space.
    c   The air is polluted.
    d   The streets are often dirty and there is lots of rubbish lying about.
    e   It is dangerous and you are scared to go out at night.
    f   There is too much noise.
    g   Life is stressful and hectic.
3   a   You have lots of space.
    b   There are nice cycle tracks and walking paths.
    c   The air is fresher.
    d   It is much quieter.
    e   The scenery is pretty.
    f   You live in the middle of nature.
    g   There is little crime.
    h   Everyone knows each other.
4   a   There is often only one shop.
    b   There is nothing to do.
    c   You feel isolated.
    d   There is no regular transport service.
    e   Life is very boring.
    f   There are few leisure facilities.
    g   My friends live far away.

 **ACTIVITY** Where I used to live

Thea used to live in the country.

Advantages: Everyone knew each other. You had a lot of freedom. You could play outside when the weather was nice as there were lots of grassy areas. The air was fresher. There was less crime.

Disadvantages: There was no regular transport service. Her friends lived far away.

Torsten used to live in the city.

Advantages: Life was exciting. There was lots to do. You could go to the cinema or ice-rink. There was a good choice of shops and pubs.

Disadvantages: His mother was often ill. She found the air too polluted. Life was too stressful and hectic.

Environment – Die Umwelt

ACTIVITY Was ist das größte Umweltproblem?

- air pollution
- water pollution
- too much rubbish
- noise pollution
- over-population
- desertification
- the extinction of species
- global warming
- greenhouse effect
- too much traffic and traffic jams on the motorway
- products with too much packaging
- the dying forests
- the hole in the ozone layer
- acid rain

ACTIVITY Protecting the environment

1 I buy environmentally friendly products.
2 I recycle glass.
3 I separate rubbish.
4 I travel by bike.
5 I compost refuse.
6 I use an eco-friendly shopping bag.
7 I use public transport.
8 I buy products with little packaging.
9 I take my old clothes to a collection point.
10 For school I buy notebooks made of recycled paper.
11 I don't throw litter on the ground.

ACTIVITY Infinitives

1 duschen
2 fahren
3 trennen
4 ausschalten
5 recyceln
6 benutzen
7 kompostieren
8 kaufen

ACTIVITY Magazine articles

Alternative Energiequellen

1. Burning coal/and oil/and from nuclear power stations. (3)
2. The amounts of coal and oil available are becoming reduced/ when you burn oil it produces carbon dioxide/nuclear power is dangerous. (3)
3. Natural energy produced by water/sun and wind/they are not going to run out/they are environmentally friendly (5)

Jeder kann was tun, um die Umwelt zu schützen

1 The school organised an environment day. (1)
2 They picked up rubbish in the town centre. (1)
3 That there was so much litter on the streets/plastic bottles, packaging and cigarette butts. (2)
4 They handed out eco-friendly bags for people to take to the supermarket. (1)
5 They handed out leaflets with tips about how to protect the environment. (1)
6 Lots of people threw the leaflet away onto the street. (1)

Elefantenart vom Aussterben bedroht

1 *Any two from:*
- type of Asian elephant
- the biggest animal on land in Indonesia
- they can grow up to 6 m long and 3 m tall
- they need a large living space

2 The forests are being chopped down for wood/they are planting fields. (2)
3 There are only 2800 elephants left in Indonesia which is half as many as 30 years ago. (1)

LEARNING

School subjects – Die Schulfächer

ACTIVITY Learning techniques – Lernmethoden

1 I learn vocabulary.
2 I solve problems.
3 I do group work.
4 I work with a partner.
5 I work on the computer.
6 I write notes.
7 I read a text.
8 I look up words in a dictionary.
9 I do research.
10 I write essays.
11 I draw.
12 I give a presentation.
13 I play an instrument.
14 I do sport.
15 I improve my listening comprehension.
16 I practise spelling.
17 I do mental arithmetic.
18 I build things.
19 I cook.
20 I learn grammar.
21 I prepare for the exams.
22 I do an experiment.

APPENDICES

⚙ ACTIVITY Teachers

a 8% = likes teaching
b 20% = has a sense of humour
c 9% = organises trips
d 12% = can explain things well.
e 4% = only gives a punishment when necessary.
f 5% = has no favourites in the class.

Preparing for exams – Die Prüfungen vorbereiten

⚙ ACTIVITY Study techniques

1 I make a study plan.
2 I study with friends and we test each other.
3 I record notes on my mobile phone.
4 I type up notes on my computer.
5 I use various study methods.
6 I do exercises online.
7 I read through my notes then my mum asks me questions.
8 I learn the most important ideas by heart.
9 I surf the internet and research a topic.
10 I read a text and then I make up questions.

⚙ ACTIVITY Preparing for exams

1 They get worried/they suffer from stress.
2 You can talk to each other
You can share ideas.
You can test each other.
You can ask each other questions.
You can send each other a text and encourage each other.
3 It is important to relax the evening before the exam. You can go for a walk in the fresh air. You can do yoga at home to calm your nerves.
It is better if you can sleep right through the night. Before you go to bed, have a bath or listen to nice music. A warm drink such as hot chocolate might help.
You should eat healthily. You should eat a proper meal and not snack. Try to eat food containing lots of vitamins.

Describing my school – Meine Schule beschreiben

⚙ ACTIVITY Describing my school

1 Deutschland
2 Deutschland
3 Deutschland
4 Schottland
5 Deutschland
6 Schottland
7 Schottland
8 Deutschland
9 Deutschland
10 Deutschland
11 Schottland
12 Deutschland
13 Schottland
14 Deutschland
15 Deutschland

⚙ ACTIVITY Karl's school

1 He has lots of friends/there are lots of clubs.
2 The compulsory subjects are Maths, German and a foreign language. He chose Art, Geography, Physics and Biology. He finds Biology easier than Physics. He doesn't like Physics as it is so complicated. The teacher gives too much homework. His favourite subject is Art because it is fun. The teacher is nice and enjoys teaching.
3 The school building is quite old. The classrooms are very small and quite dark. There is a nice library and a new gym hall. The assembly hall is awful because it is dirty and untidy.
4 There are 90 teachers. Most teachers are helpful and friendly. Some teachers are strict and impatient.
5 There are 1000 pupils. Some pupils are cheeky and lazy but most of them are hard-working and funny.
6 School starts at 8.00 and finishes at 1.15. There are two breaks. One break lasts 10 minutes and the other lasts 15 minutes.

⚙ ACTIVITY Tobias's school

1 A comprehensive school (1)
2 In a village/not far from his house (2)
3 They are compulsory subjects (1)
4 It is fun/the teacher is understanding (2)
5 It is awful/they have a lot of writing to do (2)
6 It is important for his future or he wants to study medicine at university (1)
7 The building is a bit old-fashioned/many classrooms are very small but tidy (2)
8 There is an excellent sports ground where you can play football/the library has a good choice of books (2)
9 Chess club/they have won the last four matches (2)

School rules – Die Schulregeln

⚙ ACTIVITY Margit's opinions

Rules she agrees with:
1 You are allowed to wear trainers.
2 You must switch off the computer.
3 You must arrive at school punctually.
4 You must walk properly on the stairs.
5 You must be helpful and polite.
6 You are not allowed to smoke/take drugs.
7 Knives are strictly forbidden.
8 Bullying is strictly forbidden.

Rules she disagrees with:
1 You must do homework.
2 You are not allowed to chat during the lesson.
3 You are not allowed to chew gum.
4 You must respect all pupils and teachers.
5 You are not allowed to play truant from school.
6 You must listen to the teachers.

Strange rules:
1 You must bring a pet to school every day.
2 You are allowed to eat fried sausage during the lesson.
3 You must write on the table.
4 You are allowed to behave badly.
5 You are allowed to arrive at class late.
6 You are not allowed to wear black clothes.

7   You are not allowed to learn new things.

8   You are allowed to fight.

⚙ ACTIVITY Kaugummi

1   During the lessons (1)

2   Bits of chewing gum are left under tables or on the floor. (1)

3   60% of teachers said that they were not against chewing gum. (1)

4   *Any two from:* It stops you being overweight/it relieves stress/ it keeps you awake (2)

⚙ ACTIVITY School uniform

1   T-shirts/sweatshirts/blouses/trousers/skirts (in many colours)

2   15% want to wear a uniform if it is fashionable.

3   They don't have to spend money on expensive clothes.

4   When all pupils wear a uniform, then clothes are not a status symbol.

5   Everyone looks the same/the clothes are an expression of their personality/they don't want to wear the same colour of shirt or blouse each day.

Learning foreign languages – Fremdsprachen lernen

⚙ ACTIVITY Fremdsprachen

1   You learn a lot about another culture.

2   You widen your horizons.

3   When you speak several languages, you can earn 20% more money.

4   Learning foreign languages helps you with your mother tongue.

5   You develop your memory.

6   It is necessary for tourism in Scotland.

7   It is easier to meet new people on holiday.

8   You are more tolerant.

9   You can work for an international company.

10 You have more job opportunities and you can work abroad.

⚙ ACTIVITY The benefits of learning a foreign language

1   To speak with people in other countries/to get to know their culture/languages are important for work.

2   Foreign languages are not so important because everyone in the world speaks English.

3   75% of the world's population does not speak English.

4   60% of British firms do trade in countries where no English is spoken – you have a better chance of getting a good job.

5   Travel and tourism/transport companies/technical support services for customers abroad/design of websites and brochures/finance and sales.

⚙ ACTIVITY Exchange trip to Germany

Julia – It is often said that everyone speaks English. It is not true. My partner and his family spoke little English, and I could not understand their German very well. They spoke very quickly and quite differently from my teacher. After a week, I could understand them better. You need to be patient.

Chris – The school exchange was a great experience. I practised my German as much as possible. I wanted to improve my German. I got on very well with my partner. We had the same interests and we could talk a lot about sport, music and even politics.

Rosie – I didn't think that it was good that the Scottish pupils were often together. We spoke English and I could not practise my German enough. I would rather go to Germany on my own and go to school there.

Carole – My stay in Germany was a lot of fun. I tried to read the newspaper every day. I noted down new vocabulary. I could understand my partner and her parents very well, as they spoke High German. I found it difficult to understand the gran, as she often spoke in a Bavarian accent.

Richard – Since the exchange visit I have been working more in German lessons. I have seen that it is fun to understand and speak a language. Most German pupils learn two foreign languages and have about eight hours of lessons a week – that is much better.

THINGS TO DO AND THINK ABOUT

Example answers:

1   Ich lerne Deutsch und Spanisch.

2   Ich lerne seit vier Jahren Deutsch und seit einem Jahr Spanisch.

3   Ich möchte Chinesisch lernen. Ich interessiere mich für die Kultur.

4   Ich finde es sehr wichtig, eine Fremdsprache zu lernen. Durch die Sprache lernt man auch die Kultur kennen. Man wird toleranter und es ist ein Pluspunkt für den Lebenslauf.

EMPLOYABILITY

Future plans – Zukunftspläne

⚙ ACTIVITY Next year

1   I will continue studying.

2   I will leave school.

3   I will do an apprenticeship.

4   I will go to university.

5   I will look for a job.

6   I will tour the world.

7   I will go to a technical college.

8   I will do a gap year.

⚙ ACTIVITY Future plans

1   I will leave school.

    I would like to work in a supermarket and earn money.

    I will find an apprenticeship as an electrician.

2   I will do my exams.

    If I get good results, I will go to university.

    I will study medicine.

3   I want to tour the world.

    I will visit Australia and India.

    I will find a job in tourism.

⚙ ACTIVITY Benefits of a gap year

Florian	It widens your horizons.
Gabi	You become more independent.
Jonas	You learn about a new country and a new culture.
Heike	You can learn foreign languages.

APPENDICES

Paul	You become more tolerant and open-minded.
Max	You develop your confidence.
Karl	You learn how to manage your money.
Kerstin	You can make new friends and important contacts.

ACTIVITY Gap year

1 If you are not sure what to study/if you want some freedom and time out after studying/job prospects are better.

You can switch off and relax after the exams.

You can get to see a bit of the world and get to know people from different countries.

You can gain experience.

You learn about the habits and way of life of another culture.

It is a plus point for the CV.

2 The problem is whether a gap year will be considered as an enriching experience or as a gap in the CV.

3 It is important to do something meaningful during the gap year such as voluntary work or learning new skills such as a foreign language.

4 He did not know what he wanted to study at university. He was interested in history and politics and could not decide which subject to study.

5 He has become more independent/he has more self-confidence/he hopes it will help him find a good job.

Jobs – Berufe

ACTIVITY Match up 1

1	F	3	A	5	H	7	L	9	M	11	N	13	G
2	I	4	J	6	B	8	C	10	K	12	D	14	E

ACTIVITY Which job?

1 Doctor – well-paid
2 Teacher – stressful
3 Hairdresser – easy
4 Dentist – tiring
5 Sales assistant – boring
6 Postman – exciting
7 Fireman – dangerous
8 Vet – varied
9 Engineer – difficult
10 Secretary – badly paid

ACTIVITY Sentence-building

1 Ich möchte Tierarzt werden, weil ich gern mit Tieren arbeite.
2 Ich möchte Briefträger werden, weil ich gern im Freien bin.
3 Ich möchte Mechaniker werden, weil ich etwas Praktisches machen will.
4 Ich möchte Lehrer werden, weil ich mit Kindern arbeiten will.
5 Ich möchte Arzt werden, weil der Job gut bezahlt ist.
6 Ich möchte Zahnarzt werden, weil man Kontakt zu Menschen hat.

ACTIVITY Match up 2

1	C	3	A	5	H	7	B
2	F	4	E	6	D	8	G

ACTIVITY Where do these people work?

1 Comprehensive school
2 Garage (car workshop)
3 Factory
4 Hospital
5 Shop
6 Dental surgery

Careers advice – Berufsberatung

ACTIVITY Ideal jobs

1 I would like to work with animals.
2 I would like to work with children.
3 I would like to work in an office.
4 I would like to work for an international company.
5 I would like to travel a lot and use my languages.
6 I would like to have contact with people.
7 I would like to earn a lot of money.
8 I would like to be independent.
9 I would like to work outdoors.
10 I would like to do something practical.

ACTIVITY Qualities

a 1 Sociable
2 Trustworthy
3 Understanding
4 Always punctual
5 Really patient
6 Hard-working
7 Helpful
8 Motivated and organised
9 Creative
10 Active and lively
11 Honest
12 Enterprising

b 1 geduldig, freundlich, intelligent
2 geduldig, verständnisvoll
3 fleißig, kreativ
4 aktiv, sympathisch, hilfsbereit
5 ehrlich, vertrauenswürdig, pünktlich

ACTIVITY Skills

1 Good marks in science
2 Polite and speaks clearly
3 Good knowledge of computers
4 Speaks fluent English and German
5 Lots of patience, especially with children
6 Likes working in a team; has team spirit.
7 Can listen well.
8 Can work to a deadline.

ACTIVITY: Careers leaflet

1 What is more important in the world of work? Good marks or positive qualities?

2 People who are polite and helpful.

3 Colleagues who are friendly and easy-going. They have a sense of humour.

4 Receptionist – must speak clearly, be organised and pleasant.

Plumber – can repair toilets and showers – be hard-working and honest.

ACTIVITY: Apprenticeships

1 You have to wait too long before you earn money. His brother was a student for four years and ended up having so much debt – his parents had to help out.

2 It is practical and varied.

3 You need to be independent and reliable. You need to get on with your colleagues.

4 He is looking forward to meeting the other apprentices. He finds practical work more interesting than theory.

5 He wants to own his own garage.

6 He has set a high goal but it is achievable.

Part-time jobs – Teilzeitjobs 1

ACTIVITY: What job?

1 waiter in a restaurant

2 chambermaid in a hotel

3 sales assistant in a department store

4 checkout assistant at petrol station (works at till)

5 babysitter – looks after the neighbours' children

6 delivers newspapers – works outdoors

ACTIVITY: Job adverts – Anzeigen

A: Do you like good food? Are you hard-working and motivated? Job as waiter/waitress in a family restaurant.

You must be over 16.

You will work ten hours a week.

You can eat for free in the restaurant.

You earn seven euros per hour and tips.

You need to work evenings.

B: Apprenticeship in hairdresser's

You will develop the necessary skills.

You must be polite, helpful and enterprising.

You will make appointments, wash customers' hair and work at the cash desk.

You must work Saturdays from 9am to 5pm.

You will earn 6 euros 50 per hour.

C: Do you like working outdoors?

We are looking for people to work in parks.

You must be 13–16 years old.

You must be active, honest and punctual.

You must water the plants and flowers.

You will work for one hour after school.

You must have permission from your parents.

You can work in a park near your home.

You will earn 35 euros per week.

ACTIVITY: What do you do at work? – Was machst du auf der Arbeit?

1 Verkäufer

2 Empfangschef/Kassierer/Verkäufer/Kellner

3 as above

4 Kassierer

5 Verkäufer

6 Empfangschef

7 Babysitter

8 Empfangschef

9 Kellner

10 Empfangschef

11 Empfangschef

12 Babysitter

ACTIVITY: When do you work? – Wann arbeitest du?

A: 1 Monday afternoon and Wednesday evening

2 eight hours per week

3 5 euros 60 per hour

4 train

B: 1 Saturday and Sunday

2 9am to 5pm (Sat); 12 noon to 4pm (Sun): 12 hours per week

3 6 euros 20 per hour

4 by car

C: 1 Thursday after school and Friday evening

2 six hours per week

3 7 euros 10 per hour

4 by bike

D: 1 Saturday morning and Tuesday afternoon

2 five hours a week

3 6 euros 40 per hour

4 walk to work

Part-time jobs – Teilzeitjobs 2

ACTIVITY: For or against?

1 for – you become more independent

2 for – you learn about team spirit

3 against – I am too young

4 for – you meet new people

5 against – I have too much homework

6 for – you learn about the world of work

7 against – I need to study for exams

8 against – you learn about punctuality

9 for – I want to earn my own money

10 for – you develop self-confidence

11 against – I have no time for friends

12 for – I am saving up for my holiday

13 against – I am often tired at school

14 for – I want to gain work experience

15 for – I want a great CV

APPENDICES

 **ACTIVITY** Translation

1 I work as a waitress in a café in the town centre. I make the tea and coffee and serve customers. I work three days a week and I earn 5 euros 60 per hour. I like the work because it is easy and varied. There is always lots to do. My boss is very patient and I get on well with my colleagues. I never get bored and I like talking to the customers.

2 I work as a sales assistant in a clothes shop. I help the customers. I fill up the shelves and I work at the cash desk. What I like best is that I get reductions. Sometimes I don't like my job so much because my boss is stressed and rude. I must work four times a week and therefore I have only very little free time. My part-time job is also badly paid. I earn only 5 euros 20 per hour.

3 I work as a receptionist in a hotel on the coast. I have to answer the phone and book excursions. I work eight hours every Saturday. The work is well paid because I earn 7 euros 40 per hour. I also get tips. I get on well with my boss, and my colleagues are understanding and helpful.

ACTIVITY Match up

| 1 | F | 3 | L | 5 | I | 7 | D | 9 | G | 11 | H |
| 2 | J | 4 | A | 6 | B | 8 | K | 10 | C | 12 | E |

ACTIVITY Peter's part-time job

1 He is going to Greece on holiday with friends. (1)
2 a waiter in an Italian café (1)
  b all day Saturday and Sunday afternoon (2)
3 a He likes having contact with people. (1)
  b The weather can be too hot in the summer. Some customers can be in a bad mood and are not friendly. (2)
4 He earns eight euros an hour plus tips/he is well paid. (1)
5 You become more independent/you develop self-confidence/ you get an insight into the world of work. (3)

Work experience – Arbeitspraktikum 1

ACTIVITY Where did you work?

1 office
2 factory
3 shop
4 hairdresser
5 car firm
6 vet's surgery

ACTIVITY Different work experiences

Silke

1 travel agent's
2 It was very useful.
3 She learned how to talk to customers and why foreign languages are important.

Lars

1 firm of lawyers
2 It was a waste of time.
3 The people in the office had too much to do. They had no time for him. He had to sit the whole day and watch. He photocopied documents and made the coffee.

Christina

1 in a nursery school
2 It was great fun.
3 It helped her to make important decisions about her future career. She enjoyed working with the children – doing drawing and craftwork. She also taught the children English vocabulary.

 **ACTIVITY** Stefan's work experience

1 teacher
2 wants to work with children/have long holidays
3 helpful, friendly and creative
4 in June
5 primary school
6 ten days
7 found it great
8 8am to 1pm
9 funny and nice
10 strict

ACTIVITY Fill in the blanks

möchte
arbeiten
bin
Arbeitspraktikum
habe
gearbeitet
Tage
gefunden
gefahren
Uhr
waren
war
fünfzig

ACTIVITY What were you asked to do?

1 I made coffee.
2 I photocopied documents.
3 I answered the phone.
4 I wrote e-mails.
5 I tidied up.
6 I worked at the cash desk.
7 I served the customers.
8 I worked on the computer.
9 I played with the children.
10 I organised games and trips.

Work experience – Arbeitspraktikum 2

 **ACTIVITY** Complete the passage

gemacht
gearbeitet
verbracht

gegangen

begonnen

geendet

gelernt

geschrieben

gekocht

beantwortet

gemacht

verdient

entwickelt

geworden

CULTURE

Holidays – Die Ferien 1

ACTIVITY Why do these people choose to travel?

1 to get a change
2 to escape the bad weather
3 to have a lot of fun
4 to switch off
5 to improve my foreign languages
6 to learn about another culture
7 to experience other countries
8 to get away from daily life
9 to have an adventure
10 to relax

ACTIVITY When do these people go on holiday?

1 every year
2 in the summer holidays
3 in the high season
4 in autumn
5 in the Easter holidays
6 in spring
7 in the Christmas holidays
8 at the beginning of July

ACTIVITY Why do people choose certain destinations?

1 The beaches are excellent.
2 The sun shines every day.
3 The nightlife is wonderful.
4 There is a good choice of shops.
5 There is lots to see and do.
6 There are lots of tourist attractions.
7 There is a huge water park.
8 I am interested in the culture and language.
9 The people are hospitable.
10 The food is delicious.

ACTIVITY Heike's holidays

1 In spring. (1)
2 They rent a holiday flat/with a swimming pool/and a view of the sea. (3)
3 a They go to the beach to sunbathe. (1)
4 b They meet up with relatives for dinner./They go to a restaurant and try the specialities – normally seafood. (2)
5 Advantage = the parents pay for everything

Disadvantages = less freedom/lots of rules/parents always want to know where she is going and with whom/she must be home by midnight. (4)
6 They get on well/they have the same interests/they have the same tastes/Gabi makes her laugh. (3)
7 They would go to pubs every night and/have a long lie until midday the next morning. (2)

Holidays – Die Ferien 2

ACTIVITY German holidays

1 Italy, Spain and Croatia (3)
2 63% = those who travel to the North Sea, Baltic Sea and Mediterranean.

12% = those who plan a trip to the mountains.

16% = those who stay at home and give high energy costs as the reason.

18% = those who got help from a travel agent to plan the trip. (4)
3 The towns have the best tourist attractions/but also the best entertainment/and sports facilities. (3)
4 For a change of scenery/to forget daily life, worries and problems./You don't have to do housework – no beds to make and no washing up./It is good for your health/ you can relax and convalesce./You can enjoy the sun and fresh air. (4)
5 Those who choose their holiday based on their hobby – where they can best do their activities/for example, hill-walkers, sailors, horse-riders, cyclists, anglers and divers.

Those who like to meet other people/and widen their circle of friends. (4)
6 Waiting in a queue at check-in at the airport.

The traffic jams on the motorway.

People who consume too much alcohol and behave badly. (3)

ACTIVITY Jedes/Letztes Jahr

Jedes Jahr = this year

Abends gehe ich zum Freizeitpark.

Ich gehe zum Strand.

Ich fahre mit meinen Eltern in die Türkei.

Die Leute sind freundlich.

Ich fahre mit dem Auto.

Ich bade im Meer.

Ich fahre mit dem Schiff.

Ich wohne in einem Wohnwagen auf dem Campingplatz.

Letztes Jahr = last year

Ich habe in einer Ferienwohnung gewohnt.

Ich habe Volleyball am Strand gespielt.

Ich bin mit meiner Familie nach Spanien gefahren.

APPENDICES

Es hat Spaß gemacht.

Ich habe die Sehenswürdigkeiten besichtigt.

Das Essen war lecker.

Jeden Abend sind wir in die
Disko gegangen.

Literature and cinema – Literatur und Kino

ACTIVITY War Horse

Task A

1   story
2   farm
3   sells
4   sad
5   France
6   injured
7   healthy
8   war
9   rider
10 warmth

Task B

Max	The film was scary.
Gabi	I found the film exciting.
Florian	The music was great.
Thomas	The special effects were great.
Luisa	I found the film childish.
Jonas	The film was too sentimental.
Mia	The film was very sad. I cried.
Kevin	The story was at bit strange and unbelievable.

ACTIVITY Benefits of reading

1   Reading can help with Alzheimer's disease. With regular reading, you can stay more mentally fit for longer when older.
2   You can relax. You can escape daily life and travel into the world of fantasy.
3   Reading educates. With regular reading, you can automatically widen your vocabulary.
4   Lots of people have difficulty falling asleep. They cannot switch off. When you pick up a book and read a few pages, your mind relaxes.
5   Reading has a positive effect on creativity. By diving into the world of fantasy, you develop the power of the imagination.
6   Reading widens your horizons. Stories give you an insight into the life of others, their thoughts, their work and habits. You learn about faraway places and experience foreign cultures.

ACTIVITY Anne Frank

1   For teenagers who need to overcome difficult/or dangerous situations. (2)
2   The book has been translated into 600 languages/Anne Frank's house has over 800,000 visitors a year from all over the world. (2)
3   Mia also has a difficult relationship with her sister. (1)
4   Anne writes openly about typical teenage problems. (1)
5   She believes in the good in people. She never speaks about hatred. (2)

Festivals – Feste

ACTIVITY Carnival

1   They get dressed up/they dance in the streets/they organise 'foolish' parades. (3)
2   It is to do with the spring festival of the Teutons/they believed in demons/they held a spring festival to chase away the winter spirits. (2)
3   A devil's mask/an animal mask. (2)

ACTIVITY Oktoberfest

1   It is not only a festival for the people of Munich/but also a large international event. (2)
2   The mixture of high tech and tradition. (1)
3   The original festival was organised for the prince's wedding. (1)
4   Showmen and breweries. (2)

Facts

- 6.9 million visitors.
- The breweries make a special beer with a higher alcohol content.
- 12,000 people work at the festival, 1600 of whom are waiters and waitresses.
- There are about 104,000 seats.
- On average 60,000 hectolitres of beer are drunk and 500,000 fried chickens are sold.
- There are about 1000 tonnes of rubbish.
- The approximately 6.9 million visitors spend 435 million euros in the 16 days (that is 63 euros per person on average).
- In 2014, there were 4900 lost-property items including clothes, identity cards, credit cards, wallets, mobile phones, bags and keys.

ACTIVITY Der Jahresmarkt – Fairground

1   C
2   F
3   D
4   E
5   A
6   B

COURSE ASSESSMENT: WRITING

Introduction and bullet point 1

ACTIVITY Translation

1   Hello! I am called Thomas Fletcher and I am 16 years old. My birthday is on 3 September. I live in Thurso in the north-east of Scotland. Thurso is a small town on the coast and there are about 10,000 inhabitants.
2   My first name is Julia and my family name is Brown. I am 15, but in two weeks I will be 16. I live in a small village in the country not far from Glasgow.
3   I am called Karolina Panasiuk and I will be 18 on 8 May. At the moment I am living in Dumfries, a town in the south of Scotland. I originally come from Poland but I have been living in Scotland for ten years. I like living in Scotland because the scenery is so pretty.

4   My name is Craig Finlayson and I am 17 years old. I live in a lovely area in a suburb of Aberdeen. I have lived there my whole life and I like the area because there is lots to do.

Bullet point 2: School/college education experience until now

 **ACTIVITY:** *Positiv* or *negativ*

Positiv

Ich habe gute Noten in Mathe.

Ich mache gute Fortschritte in Kunst.

Ich finde Deutsch wichtig für meine Zukunft.

Meiner Meinung nach ist Erdkunde einfach.

Negativ

Ich bin schwach in Chemie.

Ich finde Biologie schwierig.

Ich bekomme schlechte Noten in Informatik.

THINGS TO DO AND THINK ABOUT

besuche; heißt; groß; ungefähr; Lehrer; Ruf; erklären; Letztes; Pflichtfächer; mag; wichtig; Meinung; schwierig; werde; studieren.

Bullet point 3: Skills/interests you have which make you right for the job

THINGS TO DO AND THINK ABOUT

1   Ich habe die Anzeige in der Zeitung gesehen und ich möchte mich um die Stelle als Kellner/Kellnerin bewerben.
2   Ich möchte eine neue Kultur kennen lernen und mein Deutsch verbessern.
3   Ich bin sehr fleißig und ich arbeite gern in einem Team.
4   Ich habe die richtigen Eigenschaften für den Job. Ich bin höflich und vertrauenswürdig.
5   Nach der Schule möchte ich im Ausland arbeiten und meine Fremdsprachen üben.

6   In meiner Freizeit treibe ich gern Sport. Ich bin in einer Hockeymannschaft und ich trainiere jeden Samstag.
7   Wenn ich Zeit habe, mache ich sehr gerne einen Spaziergang. Es ist wichtig fit und gesund zu bleiben.
8   Ich interessiere mich für Musik und ich lerne seit drei Jahren Gitarre.
9   Meine Leidenschaft ist das Kino. Ich gehe einmal in der Woche ins Kino.
10 Wenn das Wetter schön ist, gehe ich gern auf dem Land reiten.

Bullet point 4: Related work experience

ACTIVITY What you did – was du gemacht hast

1   C
2   E
3   F
4   G
5   A
6   H
7   B
8   I
9   D

ACTIVITY Max's work experience

1   In February. (1)
2   In a primary school. (1)
3   *Any three from:* He played with the children/he corrected notebooks/he took part in the sports lesson/one day he went for a walk in the woods. (3)
4   He got on well with his colleagues/the boss was helpful and understanding. (2)
5   *Any two from:* He learned lots/he developed his self-confidence/he got his first insight into the world of work. (2)

GLOSSARY OF KEY GRAMMATICAL TERMS

adjective – a word used to describe a noun, for example big – *groß*; small – *klein*.

comparative – the form of an adjective that allows two or more people or things to be compared. We normally add 'er' to the end of an adjective to make the comparison, for example David is faster than Craig – *David ist schneller als Craig*.

conditional tense – used to describe what someone would do or what would happen, for example I would play tennis – *ich würde Tennis spielen*.

conjunction – a linking word or connector, for example and – *und*; but – *aber*.

definite article – 'the' in English; in German, *der/die/das* (when the subject of the sentence) and *den/die/das* (when the object of the sentence).

false friend – a word that looks similar in two languages but means different things in each language. For example, *Gift* is the German word for poison!

future tense – used to describe what someone will do or what will happen in the future, for example I will play tennis – *ich werde Tennis spielen*.

imperfect tense – used to describe a past repeated action, what used to happen, what was happening or what something was like in the past, for example I used to play/ was playing tennis – *ich spielte Tennis*.

indefinite article – 'a' or 'an' in English; in German *ein/ eine/ein* (when the subject of the sentence); *einen/eine/ein* (when the object of the sentence).

infinitive – this is the pure form of the verb and the way verbs are found in the dictionary. In English, the infinitive has the word 'to' in front of it, for example to play; in German the infinitive ends in -en, for example *spielen*.

irregular past participle – this is the past participle (see below) of a verb that does not follow the usual pattern. In English, this is when it does not end in -ed, for example I have <u>drunk</u>. In German, there is often a vowel change, for example *trinken – getrunken*.

irregular verb – a verb that does not follow a set pattern when it is conjugated (put in different forms in different tenses), for example to have – *haben*; to be – *sein*.

modal verb – a verb that combines with another verb to indicate mood, necessity or possibility, for example to want to – *wollen*; to have to – *müssen*; to be able to – *können*.

negative – a word that negates the verb, for example I don't smoke = *ich rauche <u>nicht</u>*; I never smoke = *ich rauche <u>nie</u>*.

noun – a word that names a person, place, thing, quality or action. Nouns are always written with a capital letter in German, for example *das Mädchen* = girl; *der Junge* = boy.

past participle – one of the past forms of a verb. In English we usually add -ed to the end of the verb (for example 'I have played'), and in German most verbs add 'ge' to the front of the stem and 't' to the end of the stem, for example *spielen – gespielt*.

perfect tense – used to describe a past completed action, for example I have played – *ich habe gespielt*.

preposition – a word that indicates where someone or something is in relation to another person or thing, for example the book is <u>on</u> the table – *das Buch liegt <u>auf</u> dem Tisch*.

present tense – used to describe what usually happens or what is happening in the present, for example I eat/I am eating – *ich esse*.

pronoun – a word that takes the place of a noun, for example 'Joe eats chocolate' can be changed to 'he eats it' – 'he' and 'it' are both pronouns.

qualifier – a word that gives more information about an adjective, for example very – *sehr*; quite – *ganz/ziemlich*.

reflexive verb – a verb where the action is carried out to oneself, for example to wash oneself – *sich waschen*.

regular verb – a verb that follows a set pattern when conjugated (put in different forms in different tenses), for example to play – *spielen*.

relative pronoun – a pronoun used to join two parts of a sentence together, for example *ich habe einen Hund, <u>der</u> Bruno heißt*.

subject pronoun – the person or thing that carries out the action of the verb, for example I – *ich*; you – *du, ihr, Sie*; he – *er*; she – *sie*, and so on.

superlative – the form of an adjective that shows the highest extent of a quality or characteristic, for example the fastest – *der schnellste*.

tense – used to indicate when the action of the verb takes place (present/past/future).

verb – a word that describes an action or state, for example I <u>play</u> tennis – *ich <u>spiele</u> Tennis*; he has a brother – *er <u>hat</u> einen Bruder*.